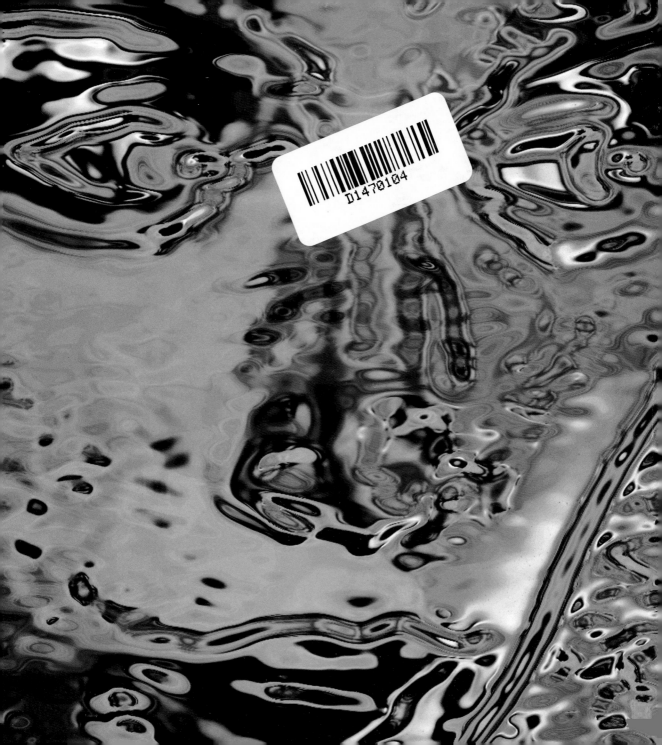

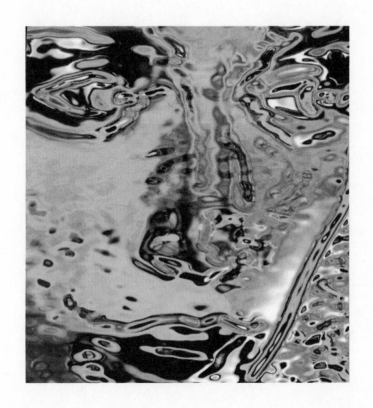

'Between the idea
And the reality
Between the motion
And the act
Falls the shadow'
T.S.Eliot

reality hacking

nicola phillips

CAPSTONE

Copyright © Nicola Phillips 1997

First published 1997 by
Capstone Publishing Limited
Oxford Centre for Innovation
Mill Street
Oxford OX2 0JX
United Kingdom

British Library Cataloguing in Publication Data<
A CIP catalogue record for this book is available from the British Library

ISBN 1-900961-10-5

Typeset in 10/13 pt Galliard and layout by
Designers & Partners Ltd, Oxford

Printed and bound in Great Britain by
T.J. International Ltd, Padstow, Cornwall

This book is printed on acid-free paper

CONTENTS

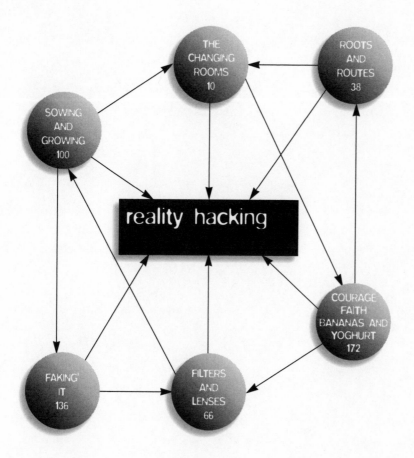

You can start or finish this book anywhere...

ACKNOWLEDGEMENTS

Dedicated to the most inspiring, supportive and unbalanced publishers anywhere in the parallel universe . . . thanks for above and beyond the call of duty . . .

Thanks to Napier Collyns for intuitive trust, proximity to food and coffee, and godfatherly behaviour. Lynn and Richard for inspiration, stimulation and connection. Ben for design and thought from the gamma quadrant. Don Michael for being both ahead of and in this time . . . I hear you. Dee, Al and Stace for warmth, love and courage under fire. Taya for strength and vision. PJ for having the most alert and sensitive aural antennae and using them to good effect.

Midnight caller, thanks for the insight and support. PG, we might still see the davidia flower. . .

A-M and Romesh for being there all the time. Linda, without whom my life would not have remained organised enough to write this.

Above all to Lauren who constantly inspires me to go with the future . . .

'Outside of a dog a book is a man's best friend.

Inside of a dog it's too dark to read'
Groucho Marx

We'd love to know what inspires you and what you think of the book.
Please e-mail Nicola and us at *capstone_publishing@msn.com*.
We can't promise an immediate reply as Nicola travels extensively
but we will answer as reality permits.

mapping the new edge

CHAOS

RISK

INNOVATION

… three words that will strike either fear or excitement in your heart. Either way, this book is about getting to grips with them. If you're frightened, the book will demystify the fear and help you go past it. If you're excited, the book will help you make the most of your excitement and put your energy where it needs to be.

We are exposed to more and more information. Perhaps, once, this would have implied more power to control our lives. Instead the more we know, the more we realise how many variables there are, and how uncertain life is. We could question more, but what we tend to do is criticise, feel helpless, or at worst distrustful. In order to deal with, or hack, today's realities, we need to be more aware of how we can surf the waves, not control them, which has been our time honoured habit.

How can we understand more about our potential, and then learn to release it?

To get the best from ourselves and others we have to maximise our personal potency. This book is about looking at all the places where potency resides; where we miss chances to use it; how we can harness it or fail to recognise it.

So, what's new in all of this? Well, probably very little: this book, is about using personal beliefs and perspectives to make change happen …

Our habits make us reach for new techniques with which to handle the ever-changing world. We have tried management by objectives, visions, new age, new wave, self-managing teams, quality and re-engineering. We spin from one solution to the next, wondering why the solutions never seem to crack the problem. In addressing the symptoms rather than the causes, we change our ideas and techniques without ever changing our beliefs and values.

How can we hack our way through the jungle of old and new, realise what is valuable to us and what is not, what to hang on to and what to let go of?

'Don't take me as an authority. I am simply expressing a very personal point of view. Nothing final about it. You have to settle all these matters for yourself'
Robert Henri

We are resilient beings who are capable of thriving and, indeed, actively seeking challenging circumstances. However, in looking to each other too much for lessons and hints, we often end up learning from the same set of beliefs and values, so nothing really changes. In this kind of cycle, we reinvent our past, not our future; reinforce old values and avoid real change and progress. We also often fail to use our individual intuitive nature and spirit. As Snoopy says: life is like a ten gear bike; most of us have gears we never use.' This book is about asking the questions that will enable us to see how to use our full potential to hack reality.

The way we live our lives, our need to deliver products, service or information, is changing. In the past we relied on structures, titles and demarcation lines. Hacking the reality of the future demands a more fluid and flexible approach. We have to work cross-culturally, cross-functionally and cross-personality ... Never have the skills of arousing and maintaining interest – motivating people to do what you need when you need it – been so important.

However, these are skills which we all think we have but, alas, we take too lightly. Those who have them do not appreciate their potential, and those who do not have them do not realise the damage they are capable of doing.

At the heart of these skills is the ability to know and be aware of self. *We* have to be the starting point for any 'solutions' to managing in this world of ours.

This is easier said than done as we spend a great deal of time trying to avoid ourselves, particularly our darker recesses.

So, inventing our future demands an embracing of chaos, innovation and risk ...

how?

The book is not about instant answers. In terms of understanding self and others, that would be a contradiction in terms. Its purpose is to enable you to make connections, understand the connections, and see what the connections might mean for you and your future.

This book has no chapters, but is divided into six key sections. They all connect with each other – as no part of inventing our future can exist in isolation – and not only connect but also get reinforced by every other part.

You can start or finish the book anywhere ...

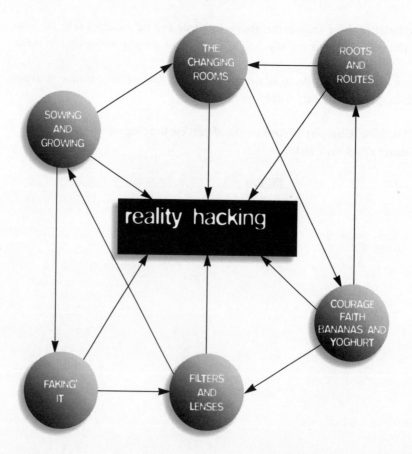

We all have a need to be able to make sense of our experiences. **Where we come from** and what we perceive as our 'home' will govern how we perceive and/or create options for the future.

*roots
and routes*

Most of us talk about **how we are going to be,** somewhere down the line and around the corner. Sometimes we even talk about ourselves as if we weren't living yet. And most of us are afraid of being who we are right now. There are issues for all of us that either open or close doors on our understanding and our future.

*roots
and routes*

The development of intelligence and consciousness has made us into reflective individuals who feel the need to interpret and to bring order to both the world of external reality and the inner world of our imagination. We need to learn how we grow, and who or what we need in order to **stimulate and sustain growth.**

*sowing
and growing*

Knowledge needs to grow into **understanding** before it becomes of use to us. The way we use language, both verbal and non-verbal, to transmit and receive, can both enable and disable awareness and progress.

*filters
and lenses*

We need to be able to have all that's left in front of us so that we can see what is really in front of us. We need to be conscious of how we respond in given situations; to understand the things, words and people that can disarm us; to know when to hold 'em and when to fold 'em. Understanding our intentions is key to **managing truth.**

*fakin'
it*

In the end we have to make sense of our own lives, however useful mentors or therapists are … this takes courage, belief and usually a **leap of faith.** It also demands knowing when to trust in the inexplicable, the irrational and the illogical. This is about soul connection.

*courage, faith,
bananas and
yoghurt*

These clouds will appear from time to time inviting you to jump from one section to another. You can jump or stay where you are – it's up to you!

This book is about understanding ourselves better in the
right now, so that we can invent the future,
and live it with fascination and excitement ...

TEACHERS OPEN THE DOOR, BUT IT
IS YOU THAT HAS TO ENTER ...

'The real trouble with this world
of ours is not that it is an
unreasonable world, nor even
that it is a reasonable one. The
commonest kind of trouble is
that it is nearly reasonable, but
not quite. Life is not an
illogicality; yet it is a trap for
logicians. It looks just a little
more mathematical and regular
than it is; its exactitude is
obvious, but its inexactitude is
hidden; its wildness lies in wait'
G.K. Chesterton

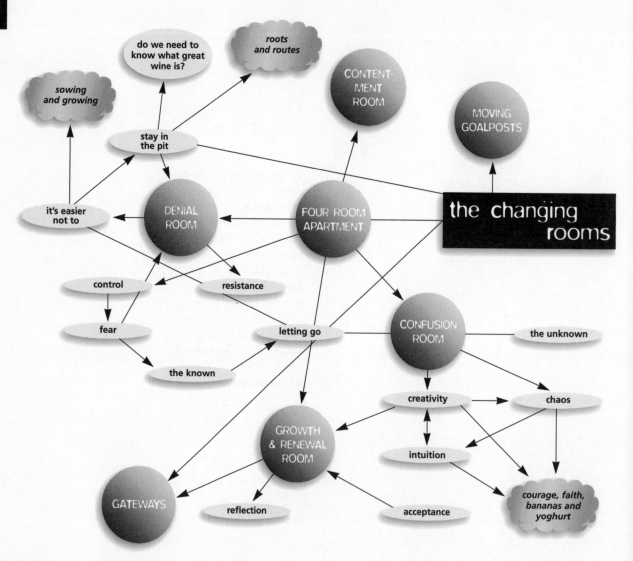

the changing rooms

'Everything should be made as simple as possible, but not simpler'
Albert Einstein

Why are we so afraid of being who we are right now?

How can we recognise and open the doors to our future?

Our lives are marked by rites of passage which we recognise either consciously or subconsciously. Some of these experiences create boundaries past which we feel unable to go, or do not want to go. They may be gateways to a different way of thinking, feeling, or being. Boundaries and gateways are neither 'good' nor 'bad', and in many ways it is hard to distinguish between the two. Hacking reality is about being aware of both our own and others' boundaries and gateways.

'It is as hard to see one's self as to look backwards without turning around'
Thoreau

# MOVING GOALPOSTS...

All of us need boundaries of some form or another.

The belief that boundaries stop us from being flexible is not just misleading, it is wrong. We actually find it a lot easier to move and be flexible when we are aware of some of our own limitations, or limitations of the situation we are dealing with. Instead of concrete boundaries, we need rubber walls so that we can bounce off and not hurt ourselves.

We always find exceptions and mistakes, so why do we still continue to seek perfection and certainty when all of our experiences tell us otherwise? We seek certainty in the world when the best we can hope for is 'the usual'.

Who creates the boundaries?

Some boundaries are societal norms, some come from our past, and some are boundaries we have set for ourselves. Knowing the difference between these three is essential to inventing our future. We need to know what will hold us back and what will open the door for us; whether they are in our minds or are a tangible reality.

Change creates boundaries and gateways. Depending on the way in which we deal with change, different kinds of boundaries and/or gateways are formed.

Every change or difference in our lives means a loss. That is, a loss of what has been. The loss might be as trivial as changing the furniture in a room, or as serious as redundancy, but a loss is what it is.

THE FOUR ROOM APARTMENT...

Loss does not just relate to bereavement. It can come from any change in our lives – losing out on promotion, moving house, missing a train.

Dealing with loss and change requires an understanding of the processes we go through every time we experience them.

Claes Jensen described the process as a four room apartment. What follows is an expanded and developed version of the original idea.

'A threat of loss creates anxiety, and actual loss, sorrow; both, moreover, are likely to arouse anger'
John Bowlby

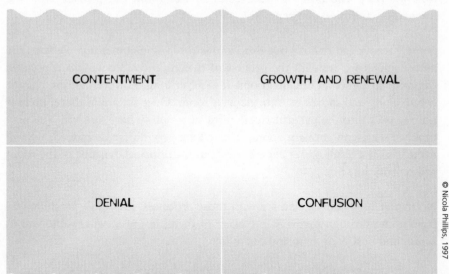

CONTENTMENT

GROWTH AND RENEWAL

DENIAL

CONFUSION

© Nicola Phillips, 1997

The apartment consists of four rooms, which we will inhabit or pass through at some point during the change process. Each room represents a particular stage of the cycle.

THE CONTENTMENT ROOM

When we are familiar with people and situations in our lives, we are sitting in the contentment room. In this room, we know exactly what the furniture looks like, we have chosen the wallpaper and the light fittings, we have our favourite comfy chair. The fire is lit, we have a warm cup of tea in our hands, and everything is cosy and safe. At work, we know exactly what is expected of us, who we report to, who we have to deal with and all the norms of the organisation.

Sometimes we don't even know we are in the room, until we have been pushed out of it by changing circumstances. At other times we don't appreciate the time for rest, reflection and recovery that this room can provide after the traumas of confusion and renewal.

Sometimes we can control our time in this room, sometimes not. Perhaps the more familiar we are with the process of change, the more we can appreciate the space in the contentment room. It is never long, however, before change comes along and moves us into the next room. Once we are in there, there is no way back into the particular contentment room we have just left. The next time we see a contentment room, it may look very different. Indeed, we will make it so as a result of our experiences, but the principal dynamic of the room will remain the same.

No matter how familiar you are with those processes, it doesn't preclude you from going through them. Being aware of them, however, will enable you to accept and deal with them and move on.

There is nothing that can take away the pain, anxiety and confusion of loss.

Don't try to!

The cycle needs to be gone through.

THE DENIAL ROOM

Once evicted from the contentment room into the denial room, every bone in our body tries to scream that nothing has changed, that everything is still the same. This prevents us having to deal with the pain of the loss. If we can pretend nothing has happened, we don't have to change anything in our lives.

So, why is the denial room so attractive?

Some of the attraction has to do with our own picture of ourselves; the self-concept. This is the essence and soul of ourselves and we therefore quite rightly, guard it closely and jealously.

It's the soft squidgy bit inside of us that we don't like anyone coming near to, and do anything we can to preserve and protect it.

For this reason we find some things extremely easy to talk about, namely those things that don't come anywhere near the squidgy bit. For example, talking about the weather, sport, other people, the theatre, is easy.

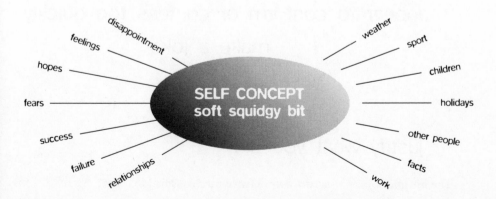

However, switch the conversation to issues which touch the soft squidgy bit, such as feelings, hopes, fears, success and failure and watch it dry up.

Whenever conversation starts around these kind of subjects, the soft squidgy bit goes into protection mode. It avoids any contact by use of defence mechanisms. These come in many different guises:

talk about someone else

change the subject

deny

lie

pretend to misunderstand

go quiet

SHOUT

discount

blame someone else

appear to conform or confess too quickly

make a joke

"yes, but ..."

"I didn't mean to ... "

justify what you did

The list goes on ... what do *your* defence mechanisms look like?

Some of the defence mechanisms are our way of coping, the only way we can handle a loss. With a loss of a partner, some people pretend the person is still there and keep their clothes in a wardrobe, waiting for them to come back. Intellectually they know a loved one has died, but emotionally the loss is too hard to acknowledge. Sometimes this way of coping is appropriate, to allow breathing space. This is very different to denying an event. We do, after all, need to protect our soft squidgy bit …

The defence mechanisms share a common trait: they all allow the individual to avoid taking responsibility for his or her own actions. If they don't own up to an action then there is nothing to change.

Another attraction of the denial room is that, from its vantage point, we can see through the doorway into the confusion room. And that is exactly what it looks like: confusion.

Sometimes we will take one step into the confusion room and feel so mixed up, that we move immediately back into the denial room, for perceived safety.

What is it we are so scared of?

Most of the time it is the unknown that we fear most; the unfamiliar. That fear will never be disposed of. We need to be able to acknowledge it, not hide from it.

The denial room is a place we have to go through. It is a room that has to be entered before we can move on. It is an essential part of the healing and growth process and therefore ignoring it or denying will inhibit growth.

Sometimes denial gets us into some pretty sophisticated patterns of behaviour. Even when you know about the process it is very easy to get caught up in the complexity of denial …

In a recent accident, my car, while travelling at fifteen miles an hour, skidded on some black ice, went off the road, over a bank, flew twenty feet in the air, came down onto a dry stone wall, progressed into a pine tree forest and finally came to rest between two pine trees.

As the windscreen and driver's window crashed in, I can remember thinking very clearly, 'OK, you have to get out of the car; but remember you are in shock, and don't try to hold it all in'. So I clambered out of the car, and scrambled up the bank sobbing my heart out.

During the two weeks that followed, virtually everyone who saw me told me how lucky I was to be alive, and I certainly agreed with them. However, what they were doing was denying to themselves how serious the accident was. The reality was that I could have died. The car, a heavy-duty four wheel drive, was a write off.

In denying the awfulness of the situation, I ended up colluding with them, as my soft squidgy bit was busy protecting itself …

The denial room was not only inhabited by me, it was also inhabited by my friends and loved ones, who also could not bear the thought of what 'might' have happened. To enable them to maintain their denials they had to keep me in the room, and of course I colluded.

What I actually needed at that moment was someone to give me permission to feel frightened, to actually acknowledge my fear both about what could have happened, and about what might happen in the future should I step into a car again.

What it meant was that I couldn't move on, and it wasn't until two weeks after the accident, that I woke up one Saturday morning and realised what I was avoiding, even knowing the process extremely well. The protection systems are so strong that sometimes they need to be nudged.

What I had not really got in touch with, what was in my confusion room, was the fear of dying; how close I had got; would I be as lucky next time, could I actually get back into a car, let alone a driver's seat?

I spent the rest of the weekend talking it out with a very supportive friend. It was not that I needed them to come up with some remarkable insight, I just needed to be able to air my fears and anxieties, without being judged, or without anyone trying to find solutions for me.

This story from the denial room is typical of the range of emotions we go through. We need to more aware of the events and behaviours that will help us out of the denial room into the confusion room, because until we get in there, there is no need for inventing a future. If we remain in denial, nothing has changed.

Take some time.

Think about your own denials.

Or those you have observed.

Go for a walk ...

Let your thoughts flow ...

THE CONFUSION ROOM

So you've finally taken a deep breath and entered the confusion room. What do you see? Well, initially very little ... it is very foggy and murky in here, and you can't make out anything. In fact, you are already beginning to feel anxious and fearful that you might never find your way out. You can't see very well, nor can you feel anything in this room. The pretence of the denial room feels very attractive in your current disorientation.

Whenever you start a new anything, expect denial and confusion. Moving yourself into the position where you can see and feel the creativity, is dependent on being able to express the fears and anxieties about the confusion room.

It means having permission to be confused, and not feeling that you are supposed to be whole and fully functional immediately following any changes in your life.

It means understanding what risk means to you or the people you are trying to support.

It means being clear about what you want, and what the change would look like for you.

It means knowing what your reality is, and what your expectations might be.

It means awareness of yourself and your limitations and the boundaries of other people.

It means making and learning from mistakes, something that is terrifying for us.

Will something terrible happen if we do it wrong?

If we have got it wrong, will we respond inappropriately?

Will our friends, colleagues and bosses think badly of us if we get it wrong?

Will we look stupid?

Answering in the affirmative to any one of those questions is likely to send us straight back into denial, but that's hardly surprising. When we are trying something new, it's hard enough without thinking we may get punished if we get it wrong. It also becomes a threat symbolising loss of control.

The anxiety of being wrong is key to personal and organisational denial. The journey through the confusion room is likely to be uncomfortable, but premature closure or conclusions will send us right back into the denial room. Too much commitment can lead to doing one thing only; too little concern produces aimless wandering. The fear of making a mistake is very strong. The need to protect oneself is so strong that we frequently search for answers before we know what the problem is, and therefore we don't have to suffer the discomfort of the confusion room. For many of us the temptation of pretence is too strong. The denial room is not a real room, but many of us pretend it is and take up permanent residence.

However, confusion is a state devoutly to be wished, not to be avoided. There is such a strong desire and conditioning that we have to be 'right' in what we do that not being able to see the way through the fog, and therefore 'see' what we have to do immediately, is terrifying.

The dictum of 'right first time, every time' is so counterproductive. Not only does it stifle innovation, creativity and risk-taking, but it prevents us from doing anything new. It is effectively permission to stay in the denial room.

Taking up residence in the denial room can only mean one thing ...

DENIAL

Nothing can or will change in the true meaning of the word; it may do on the surface, but there will be no lasting, owned, or excited, change.

Actually embracing error could be a more natural way of learning. If we could give ourselves and others permission to make mistakes, it would reduce the anxiety attached to uncertainty and the stress of being perceived to be out of control.

This is the paradox of control ...

THE ONLY WAY TO STAY IN CONTROL IS TO LET GO

Imagine yourself trying to stay in control by pulling very tightly on a rope, so that it is as taut as can be. Whilst that rope is taut, all your energies are focused on keeping it so, they cannot be put to any other, more creative use. If you pull too tightly on the rope, it may snap anyway. Furthermore, anyone can come along and cut it while you are so busy holding on.

On the other hand, if you decide when to slacken the rope, when to tighten it, and when to let go at a time you choose or think is appropriate, you are in control of that rope.

THE ONLY WAY TO STAY IN CONTROL IS TO LET GO

Think about it ...

Talking about inventing your future means accepting yourself and your situation, getting into that confusion room *and sticking with it.*

The loss of defensiveness that comes about by allowing mistakes and acknowledging uncertainty would result in more openness, understanding and supportiveness. We might even seek feedback rather than avoid it.

" *Andy had been a long-term squatter in the denial room.*

He had set up a marketing organisation with two close friends which for a while had been very successful. It had in some ways drawn them closer together, or so they thought. The cracks in the wallpaper started to show when their career needs started to diverge, and they realised that whilst a bond had been holding them together, its construction was not very solid. Several things happened at once: a few assignments fell through; one member was feeling as though all the administration of the unit was falling on her; one member became very stressed by problems with her husband; one member had reached a career crisis.

One thing all the group members had in common was an inability to share their issues with the group apart from at a very superficial level. What that looked like was each one confessing their problem very factually, then withdrawing. A dumping session. Each one had different reasons for their withdrawal, and their behaviours all looked different from the outside. They even brought in someone to help them talk through what was happening to their once happy band …

Andy was unofficially regarded as the lynchpin of the group, and was certainly seen by the outside world as such. His frustration levels with the group had been growing and growing, but he had buried them internally as he did not know how to deal with them. Indeed, he was terrified that they would explode and hurt someone.

He had a chance conversation with a new acquaintance, who did not know the rest of the group well, but who seemed to understand him. Having listened to Andy's story, he asked him why he was so frightened to tell the group what he was feeling. Andy at first replied with platitiudes about, wrong time, people had things on their minds etc. When pushed by his friend, he admitted that he was scared of being rejected by the others, and of rejection by one member of the group in particular. He also worried that if he pushed this colleague too far, she might have a breakdown.

This seemed to be a huge hurdle for Andy to jump; admitting his fears. He said very little to his friend but, two days later, after some reflection, he tackled the group about the things that were important to him. The group responded positively, including the girl whose reaction he feared.

What he had needed to do was to get his thoughts out of his head and onto a metaphorical table where he could see them in perspective. He needed no more help than this: he knew what had to be done. His journey through the confusion room just needed some support.

Most of our exciting discoveries about self and others will come while we are in the confusion room. That cannot happen in any other room.

'A more relaxed tentativeness could replace hard driving, compulsive forwardness'
Don Michael

TOUGH TASK ... SO, BOLDLY GO ...

So what else helps on the journey?

It is likely that some support will be required.

Giving support without patronising or devaluing the other is difficult for us to do. Receiving help without resisting or feeling in debt or submissive is just as difficult. Experiencing and being aware of these difficulties makes it easier to be on whichever side of the fence we happen to be, but it never makes it easy.

Whenever we offer support, there is always a fear that we might be rejected, which seems a real fear, when we understand that the individual who accepts help is anxious about either being dominated, or having their request denied or belittled. Many of us will not take the risk of offering or receiving support to avoid these experiences.

Learning to give and accept support is a prerequisite for travel through the confusion room.

courage, faith, bananas and yoghurt

This learning only takes place through a combination of positive experience and courage and intuitive leaps of faith. It is not only necessary for the confusion room, but also for understanding self better.

We learn to understand ourselves in relationships with others.

The more we understand ourselves, the more we understand people.

The more we understand people, the more we understand ourselves.

If there is no opportunity to express the feelings resulting from the circumstances that elicited them, the feelings will be displaced somewhere else. We need to express the emotions that we have in direct response to the incident or person who aroused them.

If we don't treat feelings as part of a response or message, or treat them as though they shouldn't be, we don't engage positive feelings and we can't constructively air the negative feelings in a way which allows us to choose priorities and alternatives. When feelings are excluded, consciously or unconsciously, commitment, excitement and willingness to risk go out of the window. In extreme cases, the depression that sometimes arises in our irritation at not following our feelings, gets projected outward on to the people or circumstances we believe to be responsible for ignoring our feelings. Whatever happens, if feelings are ignored, distrust increases and creativity and learning are inhibited: no chance of inventing a future in that frame of mind ...

Some people and organisations are so keen to avoid the mess of the confusion room that they add extensions or portacabins to the denial room, and set up home there.

Organisations get really subtle. So terrified are they by the confusion room that they put in huge programmes like Business Process Re-engineering, Total Quality, Training Needs Assessment and so on, and these act as a pseudo-growth room. One of the reasons these programmes frequently fail is that they never address the issues of the confusion room, namely the fears and anxieties about change and loss, both their own and their staff's. The organisation's fear is that it might not be able to change – just like any individual it is scared of the unknown. So the organisation effectively wallpapers over the door to the confusion room, and moves into its castle in the air.

David was the human resources director at a large multinational corporation. He had already been on the receiving end of one very disruptive and demotivating restructuring process, and was determined that in his new organisation, he would not let it happen.

When the inevitable missive arrived from the 'board', he was ready with his plan of action, list of working parties, and addresses of consultants. He even brought in one consultant to train the senior managers to deliver bad news, and offer a support service for his personnel team.

He put all his systems in place, but did not allow for any slippage in his programme. When the consultant in charge of the Business Process Engineering Project went over budget, he was terrified that he would have no system to 'make change'. In order to fund further work in this area, he cut what appeared to be the 'soft' option: he cancelled the training and support for his team, and cut short the work on delivering bad news.

What he was left with was a system, but nothing to help people through it. He had no way of dealing with the issues and feelings that the programme would generate. His chances of pulling it off were minimal. However, the denial room was calling him, and the pretence of doing something was overwhelming.

The end result was a lot of heartache both for David and the members of the organisation. Four out of his team of seven staff resigned or left because of stress levels. They could not deal with the amount of disturbance generated by the restructuring, neither did they have the time factored in to their working days to support either the employees or each other.

David shielded himself from what was going on by developing new additions to the system, and not relating to his team. He even managed to shut out the fact that he had lost over half his team. It was not until the rest of his team threatened to resign that he had to recognise what had happened.

He had generated a pseudo-change room in the denial room, and getting out of it would have meant confronting his fears, anxieties and, to a large extent, his guilt.

He told everyone that he felt his work was done in the organisation and looked for and found another job. It is very possible that this part of his life will forever remain a denial room for him.

This story does not have a happy ending for either David or the people involved with him. It is, however, a typical tale from the denial room …

So, how long can you stay in the denial room? Pretty well permanently if you so desire … we normally do it without knowing or owning up to it. And what are the consequences of staying there? The bottom line is that you never really change or grow, with all the feelings and emotions that might bring. Actually acknowledging that you don't want to change and that you will accept the consequences of that decision is not denial, if you really mean it.

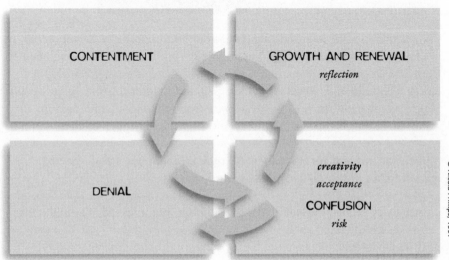

CONTENTMENT

GROWTH AND RENEWAL
reflection

DENIAL

creativity
acceptance
CONFUSION
risk

© Nicola Phillips, 1997

Sometimes the things we cling to in our desire to stay safe are the very things that keep us unsafe – the icons of safety become albatrosses around our necks.

'The most terrifying thing is to accept oneself completely'
Jung

For many people, survival, safety, security, belonging and recognition are far more important goals than self-fulfilment. If we do not perceive that inventing our own future is going to enable us to feel 'safe' or, worse, may lose us any of these goals, then there is no way we will enter the confusion room. Indeed, why should we?

However, this is a perception, and not necessarily a reality. The only way we will believe that we are still 'safe' is by taking that leap into confusion and experiencing what it really means to us. It's like trusting people. No one will trust anyone because they are told to, or are told they can. (Trust me, I'm a doctor/accountant/management consultant …)

The only way we learn to trust is by experiencing it. That can take a while, and will inevitably, at some point, involve a leap of faith in something or someone. Inventing your own future means learning to trust yourself …

courage, faith, bananas and yoghurt

We sometimes stick to a particular behaviour because of its familiarity to us. If we know what an outcome will be, no matter how unpleasant, it is sometimes preferable to us than something new, even if there is a chance it might feel good. The unknown seems always less preferable to the known. Some people repeat particularly distressing behaviours from childhood, not because they enjoy them, but because at least they know what will happen to them.

Organisations and individuals stay stuck in behaviours and systems because they are familiar with the outcomes.

Leaving a situation, whether it is a relationship, job or specific pay and reward system holds the same terror: I may be unhappy now, but at least I know what that unhappiness looks like.

What would being happy look like?

For many individuals, finding themselves in this situation is so frightening that they have to invent stories to maintain a familiar position.

Diana is very capable and bright. She had spent most of her life trying to please people, and only felt comfortable when she was doing what she perceived others wanted. This was true not only in her job, but also in her relationships. Finally, someone came along and offered her what she thought she had always wanted – a relationship in which she would be cared for no matter what she was, or how she behaved.

After the first flushes of happiness, she was thrown into total confusion. She could not understand why she was beginning to destroy the relationship. Actually she was not in the confusion room at all – she had sneaked back into denial. The thought of being happy was too much for her. How would she be able to deal with that? Being accepted was what she had always wanted but, once she had it, instead of talking it through and admitting how scary it was, she panicked and literally ran away.

She had not worked through what was reality and what was fantasy, and ran back to the perceived safety of denial.

This is where a boundary can either become a gateway to the future or a locked and barred door that keeps us trapped.

There are times in life when we have to accept that nothing, however wonderful, will make us feel great, so we might as well stay down there, and feel the pain and confusion. Sometimes having the experience allows us to recognise it for what it is the next time; that it is part of our journey, part of the future we have created, part of what we do.

Sometimes we need to feel bad: even allowing ourselves to do that actually empowers us.

**This is how issues move from being
barriers to gateways.**

Letting go can take away the overwhelming feelings of helplessness.

Lurking in the far corner of the misty confusion room is a curtained off section which is dimly lit. There we discover the creativity that is necessary to get into the next room. The excitement that comes from the energy that we generate in this part of the apartment, can only be tapped if we have gone through the maelstrom of confusion. Just before the creativity area is the place we reach when we accept our reality and acknowledge what it means for us.

The ability and energy comes partly from the sense of achievement we have from having got through the pain and discomfort. At this point the curtains part, the light brightens and we can begin inventing ...

This moment of discovery is very powerful but, in our excitement, we need to find a way to acknowledge where we have come from and what we have been through: not to dwell on it, but to feel the achievement of having struggled up the mountain. When you're struggling down at the bottom it is hard to believe you'll ever reach the summit, and sometimes the relief is so great, that all we want to do is move on.

If we can hold that moment, we might remember it for the next time.

It is a key part of our growth process …

Hold the moment …

Generating ideas at this point in the cycle is like falling off a log.

They flow so fast that the only problem you have is catching them all.

The only danger is that you can still opt for premature conclusion by taking the first idea.

You have been through so much, that you can afford to spend a little more time without resolution …

At least at this point, you know there is going to be something you can do. Enjoy the excitement of the flow of ideas for your future …

THE GROWTH AND RENEWAL ROOM

The first thing we do in this room, having got there via the creativity of the confusion room, is pause and reflect on what we are doing. We need time to take stock and appreciate what we have been through and achieved before we settle down. Having the time to reflect is an important part of growing. Here we breathe a sigh of relief, smile to ourselves, and survey our new domain ...

Most people and organisations would like to go from the contentment room directly to the growth and renewal room, without the pain of the confusion room. As we have seen, there is no growth without that journey.

Once we have got into the growth and renewal room, we don't go back to the confusion room; the door is one way. From there it is but a short step to the contentment room, and in a very short space of time, what was new becomes just the furniture and curtains. We become familiar with our situation. Then the whole process starts again.

How do we know what room we are in?

**OFTEN WE DON'T KNOW –
OR WE FOOL OURSELVES**

There are no easy answers, but the more aware we are, the faster we move and more we gain from the journey.

GATEWAYS

Most of us spend a long time in denial, or we wander through the door into the confusion room, feel awful and run back into denial. That would be a very normal process. The only door that works both ways is the door between denial and confusion. (That is if you don't board it up.)

We cannot learn very much if our defences are up and our vulnerability is avoided. If we seek to deny or control, we close the doors to growth, and certainly to any hope of inventing our future. The gateway to reality hacking lies in our ability to embrace ambiguity and all it brings. This will not change our world, but it will allow us to affect it ...

We can set and get through boundaries with a few guidelines:

live with and acknowledge uncertainty

allow mistakes, in fact, positively welcome them

accept responsibility for the effect we have on others

evaluate the present in the light of the future

accept and live with role and situational ambiguity

be open to changes in commitments and direction

Being in nature emphasises that each of us is unavoidably linked to and dependent on nature (including other people) and that the rest of nature is dependent on each of us. Given this mutual dependence, humans must be as responsible as they can be about their part in creating their own futures. But since humans are only a part of nature, what happens in the future is only partially a result of present actions. On the one hand, humans cannot expect the future to go as they would wish unless they try to guide it. On the other hand, they cannot expect the future to go the way they wish just because they try to guide it. Hence it is our responsibility to try to create a responsive future, but we cannot expect to succeed as we could if we were really in control – that is, if we were outside nature. This appreciation would make change and instability seem a more "natural" human condition because humans would not see themselves as isolated from nature – that is, conquering, or overcoming, or breaking through it'
Don Michael

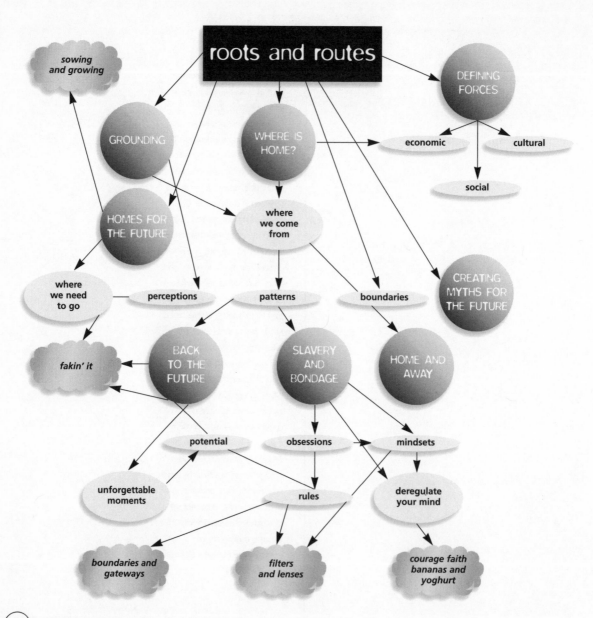

roots and routes

sowing and growing

DEFINING FORCES

GROUNDING

WHERE IS HOME?

economic

cultural

social

HOMES FOR THE FUTURE

where we come from

CREATING MYTHS FOR THE FUTURE

where we need to go

perceptions

patterns

boundaries

fakin' it

BACK TO THE FUTURE

SLAVERY AND BONDAGE

HOME AND AWAY

potential

obsessions

mindsets

unforgettable moments

rules

deregulate your mind

boundaries and gateways

filters and lenses

courage faith bananas and yoghurt

roots and routes

'We had the experience but
missed the meaning'
T.S. Eliot

When we invent our future where do we start from?

How can we use our past, our roots to help create routes for the future?

Reality hacking demands knowing when to accept your past as a reality and begin to invest in the future — but not necessarily in the past's image.

We exist in many contexts in our lives — as children, parents, managers, artists, vacuum cleaners — but underneath each of the different hats we wear, we are the same person. We may adapt our style or focus, but the base we work from is the same. Understanding this 'base' means looking at and understanding what we are comprised of, how our experiences have shaped us, and how this impacts on our ability to invent our futures.

'An elementary particle is not an independently existing unanalysable entity. It is, in essence, a set of relationships that reacts outward to other things'
H.P. Stapp

WHERE IS HOME?

Where we come from determines where and how we move forward in our lives and work.

We are tied to the context of our upbringing, social life and groupings, which help to define and give meaning to each individual's existence.

We develop notions and pictures of what 'home' feels like, or felt like, and then spend our lives either painstakingly recreating this vision, or making damn sure we do not recreate it.

If change is perceived as being threatening to our 'social life space', then we will take steps to safeguard our environment.

> **On a good day, this might mean determining new ways of evaluation and self-definition.**

> **On a bad day, we revert to the norms which are most familiar and therefore offer the most gratification.**

'Neither an individual nor a society can be reset to zero, wiping out what has happened and the effort to wipe it out'
Don Michael

When the French describe preferential conditions for grape growing, they use the word, '*terroir*'. This describes all the natural conditions that affect the biology of grapevines and the grape itself: the convergence of soil, climate, landscape, temperature, hours of sunlight, rainfall, and dozens of factors that come 'magically' together through controlled and uncontrolled processes. Together they produce a distinctive product.

To hack our reality, we need to design and perceive personal (or organisational) *'terroir'*.

What are the different factors that create our 'terroir'?

What are the controlled and uncontrolled processes that will produce what we want?

Home is composed of realities and fantasies, values and beliefs, rituals and habits. Understanding them and the effect they have is key to creating a route to our futures.

Why do we create these realities? We need boundaries to 'keep threat outside, and support inside'. The systems we are accustomed to, or create, determine our legitimacy, power and access. They define ourselves, whether 'ourselves' is an individual, a group, an organisation or a state.

Some people and organisations are aware of their defining areas, others less so. In the macro picture, issues like 'is the man the breadwinner in relationships?', 'is a wife only there to raise children?', 'are corporations the premier social structure rather than governments?' challenge and confuse our perceptions and beliefs.

When we find out government has lied to its populace what happens to the belief system of the people?

When an organisation regarded by its employees as safe, secure and caring, starts to downsize, what happens to the values of the staff?

When a partner betrays the trust of a partner, what happens to the relationship?

These are all examples of the breaking of boundaries. If new boundaries are not set, we feel we have lost our root system.

What is our grounding?

Who gets to set the new boundaries and routes?

Instead of tackling the root causes, we seem to lurch from crisis to crisis, applying plasters. Even when we seek a change, it normally tries to reinforce the old system, even if times will not support it. Most human beings still prefer to believe and do things as they have always been done. Survival has always depended on our ability to know and conform to local rules and norms.

Paradoxically, change demands a certain level of psychological security, usually at a time when we feel at our most vulnerable.

Our belief that we are independent individuals sometimes prevents us from seeing how much our beliefs and behaviour are shaped by what we have experienced. Jesuit priests say that you can give them a child at the age of seven and they will show you the man. This shows how strong the belief is that our habits of a lifetime are determined at a very early age, both by our genetic inheritance and our cultural environment.

Having a 'home' is not a negative thing …
… we just need to understand whether or when our needs and requirements change, and how we need to adjust our new 'home' accordingly.

DEFINING FORCES...

So what are the defining forces of 'home'?

Who defines them?

When do they get defined?

Can we re-define them?

The answer to the last question has to be yes ... but first you have to know what the original definition is, so that you know what it is you are re-defining. We need to know where we come from before we can define our future, otherwise we may meet the same obstacles on the new paths we draw.

When situations are familiar to us and conform to known experiences, we feel 'at home'.

We have many concepts of familiar systems and stable relationships. We have few, if any concepts or pictures of turbulent or complex situations. If we cannot see them as part of our 'home', then of course they cannot be part of a route to the future. We need to develop ways of dealing with incoherence, and acknowledging it as part of our lives.

Each of us has had defining forces in our lives, and to a greater or lesser extent they will be the forces that we instinctively turn to when defining our future.

'In an era of widespread social turbulence, the efforts of individuals and institutions to assert and exercise control over societal circumstances are increasingly seen to be counterproductive. A different perception of the nature of existence, and a recognition that inability to control is not necessarily a sign of weakness or incompetence, could help nourish the emergence of more humane and worthy modes of personal behaviour and public regulation'
Don Michael

41

Each of these forces may take a prominent role in life-making decisions at different times in life.

These forces can be divided into major groups:

Individual or genetic forces which we are born with ...

What are your defining forces: what makes you you?

Family cultures ...

What were the defining forces in your family?

What do you think their impact has been on you?

Religious roots ...

What were and are your religious or spiritual defining forces?

National and societal characteristics ...

How has the place in which you live(d) defined your 'home'?

Cultures define our response to situations. Sometimes we hide behind them, but most of the time they are a very real force.

Ed Schein defined a culture as a shared set of tacit assumptions that have been learnt through group experience and that have solved the internal and external problems of the group. Well, they probably did solve the problems of the time; it is hard to see how they are helping us at this point in our development.

What effect does our society have on defining our home?
(And thence on our ability to invent our futures?)

It feels like the role of government has been replaced by the role of corporations. In a transnational world, the corporation has become the premier social structure. In many cases it defines and decides economic and social futures.

So where does that leave the individual? If you do not have a 'job', how do you get on the track of having a future at all, let alone inventing your own?

Arie de Geus has a theory that initially land and the possession thereof was the source and indicator of economic success. Then the source moved to capital. Now he suggests that the source and indicator is information.

Those who have the access to information have the power to succeed.

What happens to those who do not have access?

What will they do?

CREATING MYTHS FOR OUR FUTURE...

We all share certain unquestioned beliefs about purposes of life that are right and worth maintaining.

These are the underpinning mythologies of our culture.

The so-called 'information society' challenges many of these mythologies. In the West, issues that we perceive to be 'natural and right' – such as freedom of speech, science, individuality, a 'Christian' god, male dominance – are the precepts and myths govern our expectations of society.

In recent history, many of these myths have been challenged: is it really 'a man's world'?; what does a 'Christian' god mean in a multicultural society? These mythologies may or may not be desirable, but they are no longer the only options.

The information age has exposed us to many options, which does not always make life easier. Uncertainty is a trademark of the information society. The more information we have, the more we see that we need more information, whether it is regarding economic futures, the greenhouse effect or personal growth. Sometimes we even question the sources of the information. So adjusting to the new routes means taking the information and using it to help us develop new myths and processes, rather than the information itself being the myth.

How can governments, educators, parents and individuals manage this psychological assault on perceived roots?

So how do we utilise these pictures from the past to try to create a future?

Having to choose between the alternative future scenarios we create will sometimes cause us problems; we feel as though we will lose something in the choice. Our choices are also only as good as the freedom we have allowed ourselves in creating the scenarios. How we create these stories or piece things together is not always clear to us. That makes it hard to duplicate or even understand sometimes.

Unless we can find a way of framing our roots in our new reality, frustration and anxiety will inhibit the invention, vision and innovation that could develop from this new route …

We need to seek resilience rather than control, and to greet the new routes, rather than see them as a challenge to our old roots.

In our complex world, there can be no single cause, and therefore no single cure. In a resilient world, by contrast to a controllable one, things can be adjusted, within constantly moving, fluid bounds, for a time, but not permanently.

LEARNING HAPPENS IN TURBULENT TIMES, PERSONAL AND HISTORICAL

We all need to learn how to learn in our own fashion.

'Our lives are ceaselessly intertwined with narrative, with the stories we tell and hear told, those we dream or imagine we would like to tell, all of which are reworked in that story of our own lives that we narrate to ourselves in an episodic, sometimes semiconscious, but virtually uninterrupted monologue. We live immersed in narrative, recounting and reassessing the meaning of our past actions, anticipating the outcome of our future projects, situating ourselves at the intersection of several stories not yet completed'
Peter Brooks

'I want to spend my time talking positively about what's true, and if that threatens anybody or their beliefs that's their problem'
Richard Dawkins

45

SLAVERY AND BONDAGE ...

Our values determine what constitutes a 'problem', 'opportunity', 'challenge', and our ways of responding to them. If we want to change our responses, then we at least need to know and understand our values; what we are prepared to do and what we are not prepared to do. How far will we go? Where are our lines in the sand?

This is no easy task given the complexity of choice we are faced with; the multiple courses for action; the confusing and uncertain signals. How do we interpret them and choose how to act?

WE FIRST NEED TO KNOW WHERE WE COME FROM, AND WHAT WE WANT

Q: *What are we in bondage to?*
A: Voices from the past, addictions, cultural messages from the environment, myths, success.

Q: *Who are the slavemasters of the bondage?*
A: I'm afraid we are. We allocate the role to various different people or organisations in our lives, but it is we who make the allocation. All major religions provide a diagnosis of the human condition, and a prescription for the cure. Taking the prescription in its own way can become bondage.

The dynamic tensions involved in managing these sometime competing forces is enough to drive anyone to distraction, panic and consequent inertia. In most Western societies the 'job' is perceived as a huge part of our lives, and for some it is considered bondage.

How do we perceive those without a job or ourselves in the wrong one?

What does that do to our inner notion of 'home'?

A perceived driving force no longer exists.

In its most serious form, what happens when you have none of those perceived defining forces? That is, you are homeless (literally), you have no family or work, and feel cut off from the society you are living in because you do not seem to have a place in it.

Is this what some of the young people in inner cities feel? With no future that they feel part of, cut off from access to work, love, community …

We all seem to have a need for a 'home'. Without that connection, we experience a loss of meaning and vitality. The notion of what 'home' is changes for us at different times in our lives, and our behaviours seem to image that notion. Defining 'home' starts us on our route forward on the journey to inventing our future.

Sometimes it feels as if we are slaves in bondage to our defining forces, whether they are political and economic, cultural or personal. These then become the ties that bind rather than the ties that enable. Overstating the importance of systems, structures and processes takes away the power and feeling from honest communication with people.

fakin' it

They can deny spirit and courage and create a society which is mechanistic, cannot take risks and does not recognise potential.

courage, faith, bananas and yogurt

47

'Scientific Management' brings with it the opportunity for supreme denial — in the form of TQM, BPR, 'value-based management', creativity programmes. They appear to satisfy needs, but it all feels over simplistic, and they all cure symptoms, not causes; they are just band aids. They also allow for the growth and development of cynicism, another denial, but also a control mechanism which keeps genuine passion under control.

Within organisations this happens with training programmes — the word programme itself seems to signify something pre-ordained with no place in it for the individual. In the same way, the project planning approach to mountaineering reduces it to a task, and misses the primitive, powerful and spiritual nature of 'mountain' and what we can experience rather than control. You remain a slave to systems rather than a person enjoying and experiencing …

We do not need to be in bondage to these systems, but nevertheless we sometimes cheerfully invent them. If an organisation or parent has shaped your life, than it is hard to give yourself permission to do something different or even be accepted.

Breaking free of other people's systems is often important if we are to grow in our own. While we are still locked in someone else's world, we cannot invent our own, but only perpetuate theirs.

HOME IS NOT ALWAYS
SOMETHING WE HAVE
IT MAY BE SOMETHING
WE HAVE LOST …

The safety of a past home is hard to leave.

Anne had worked for twelve years for a large corporation. Her working life had been structured, focused and successful. She was highly rated by her manager and colleagues.

But Anne felt she was not fulfilling her potential. Like many at her level she could not see how she had anything to offer outside the organisation. The company structures were safe — the world outside was uncertain and forbidding.

She was co-opted onto a team charged with implementing an organisational restructuring. Her job was to ensure the operation ran smoothly. With an outside consultant she developed a training package to help senior management deal with the fall out from the restructuring, specifically job loss amongst their staff.

On the day of the restructure she was called into the office of her senior manager who began to give her the speech she herself had prepared — the speech explaining that the person was being made redundant. She was stunned having had no inkling as she worked on the project that she too was one of its victims. She left that day, in a state of shock.

'Leaving home' and 'being thrown out of home' have very different effects. For some time she struggled with the loss and rejection by throwing herself into other activities. A friend recommended she apply to a consulting firm, which she did, and to her amazement was hired. She had become so used to, and dependent on 'home' she had lost faith in herself and needed the jolt of redundancy to get her to leave. Five years on she is successful again but when similar moves were announced in her new company she felt very different about leaving — 'home' was now inside of her. Leaving her job would not now mean leaving home.

Reality hacking does not mean leaving 'home' forever,

it just means acknowledging it as the place

we have come from, but not necessarily a place we have to stay.

Inventing our future is about defining the routes from one home

to another, and understanding

that we may have many along the way.

Knowing this can make it easier to leave one,

as we know we will create another.

BACK TO THE FUTURE ...

When we take photos

do we take them

of people or scenery?

Why do we take them?

What memories do they invoke?

Is it to capture

the moment

or to tie it down?

'I compared these various happy impressions with one another and found that they had this in common, namely, that I felt them as though they were occurring simultaneously in the present moment and in the distant past ... the sound of the spoon against the plate, or the unevenness of the flagstones, or even the peculiar flavour of the madeleine ... went so far as to make the past coincide with the present, leaving me uncertain in which period I was. In truth, the person within me who was at this moment enjoying this impression enjoyed in it the qualities which it possessed that were common to both an earlier day and the present moment; and this person came into play only when, by this process of identifying past with present, he could find himself in the only environment in which he could live, that is to say, entirely outside of time'
Marcel Proust

It is actually very difficult to re-experience the feeling we had at a particular moment in time. It becomes important to experience it and know it when it happens, rather than try to capture it. If you are taking photos, the experience will be less than if you just enjoy the moment because your mind's focus is on the camera.

In this way we miss so much ...

This does not only apply to the magnificent positive moments.

Our lives are also by defined by the negatives and disasters;

they, too, are part of us.

the changing rooms

Remembrance and regrets are part of our reality. They are harder to stay with for obvious reasons, but to deny them is to deny our life experience.

Experience is not the same as enjoyment, but the appreciation of one leads to the other.

Actually being able to recall moments and experiences is a part of our defining process, but we often let the systems and processes override them in our need to categorise and box things.

How can we hold on to the moment?

How do we know when a moment is going to become a defining force?

We are often so intent on moving on, on achieving the tangible, that we miss the things which actually form the core of our being. Many of our deepest values are formed by memorable moments, which we sometimes recognise as such, sometimes not. Sometimes they are formative; sometimes milestones on a journey; sometimes markers for the future; sometimes they're connections to the past.

The reality hacker needs to be aware of these moments, as they are often either turning points or signals, or indicators of what is or was important to us. Becoming more aware of what is going on around us, and the things and feelings which formulate our world is essential to inventing our future.

These moments may be held in a piece of music, a photograph, a memory of time past; it could be anything.

These moments share some common traits:

they are quite often hard to describe because they feel
so simple that we almost cannot believe that they
could have an effect (for example, the taste of a particular
cup of coffee in a certain cafe)

thinking of them usually makes us smile involuntarily

they give us a sense of well-being and warmth

recalling them can change our mood

You can see that these moments could have tremendous power in terms of opportunities to inspire both self and others in reality creation.

Being aware of and alert to these moments enables us to connect with our deepest thoughts, and therefore be more in touch with what has been, and what we really want from our reality ...

We don't see or experience them if we don't have the time or
inclination.

HOME AND AWAY ...

We don't just learn from our own experiences; we often copy the actions of others. We may avoid what seems to distress others, even if it does not threaten us personally. The origin of not walking under ladders and other superstitious behaviour may be lost in the mists of time, but the cultural transmission continues.

We need to establish our relationship with immediate space before we can extend our understanding and relationships outside of that narrow sphere.

Just as a child learns to move limbs and their relationships to objects, so we need to understand things that are close to us. Once we have done that, we can begin to assemble a network of relationships and directions between the relationships. Only then can we explore new possibilities. This is why understanding our immediate surroundings and 'home' is so important.

If we cannot understand something so close to us, how can we understand or know how to get the most from more faraway experiences? Children first see the world as centred around themselves and, even in adolescence, they are still trying to improve their ability to see how things appear from different viewpoints. Some of us never make the transition, but remain 'self-centred'. With that viewpoint, it is easy to decide your future, but hard to make it happen, because the world is composed of different people's perspectives and needs, and if we do not take them into consideration, inventing the future will remain at the policy stage. We may even bemoan the fact that we can't do anything about our lives, when actually we couldn't while trapped in the unreality of our personal universe: real to us, but not to anyone else.

Peter Drucker has compared current corporate management to conducting an opera: the conductor has a large number of different groups that he has to pull together: orchestra, dancers, chorus, soloists. They all have to come together in a common scene, in the right places at exactly the right time.

The reality hacker needs to be able to do the same with the components of his or her life.

They shouldn't be boxed or judged, but used at the appropriate time.

We need to be able to improvise, but from a basic score.

Although they are always working from a basic score or script, hackers need to be able to improvise and/or rewrite the score as they perform ...

GROUNDING ...

Why do people put in sixty to eighty hours a week to buy very fast cars in which they spend hours stuck on the freeway?

Even the wacky inspirational people in life who seem to have no need for relationships still have a need for counterpoint. Richard Branson has his hot air balloons.

How easy is it to live continuously on rocket fuel?

At 190% gravity?

**And, if you do live continuously on rocket fuel,
do you burn out quicker but brighter?**

Is that positive or negative?

Does it matter if that is the definition you have chosen?

**What would be the things you would grab if
fire broke out in your house?**

What things are irreplaceable for you?

**Who has the right to say whether the path you choose
is right' or 'wrong'?**

Well I did say that this book would raise more questions than give answers ... All these questions are not just about our defining forces, but about the things which are both outside of the limits of our homes, and those things which keep us attached to our 'homes'; the things which ground us and allow us to do the more esoteric things in our lives.

Sometimes it is people that keep us grounded, sometimes it is certain experiences.

How do we balance the two, so that we have enough stimuli and new experience to excite us, but still keep us attached to something safe?

Quite often the artificial 'homes' we create or allow to be created for us stop us doing what we really want to do. Interestingly enough it seems we can reach further and stretch ourselves more if we are grounded, whatever that grounding looks like.

So what about the power of place? Our surroundings seems to play a huge part in grounding. However, it is important to strike a balance between grounding and barriers.

We do not need to be held in bondage to our past; it exists and is part of us, but should not keep us from our future. Actually *it* doesn't, *we* do.

'Home' is about 'grounding'

What things or people make you feel safe?

Can you invoke them?

Are you dependent on them?

Are they inside you?

Small things mark the paths you have taken or might take in your life, and as such define you as an individual.

They could be a love of gardening, climbing, obscure fungi ...

Physical space, relationships routines, historical links, continuity; they all help you stay in touch with self, or perceived self.

Nina left her first marriage determined to create some safe space for herself that would not be violated by a relationship. She found her own house and started a relationship, unconsciously looking for the 'grounding' she felt she needed both in the relationship and the bricks and mortar. The ensuing relationship lasted seven years, and at the end of it Nina had the beautiful safe space she had always craved, except it was only bricks and mortar.

When the relationship ended, she initially felt grounded in her 'safe home'. However, it took a spell of travelling for her to realise that she could feel safe anywhere, as long she had the things that were truly important to her: people who cared for and respected her, and she gave herself permission to be herself.

To be herself she did not need the definition of the house. That was just a representation of the 'safety of the moment', and was not the real grounding. That was inside of her.

We all need to discover our grounding and the safety within; what defines our true selves, not the trappings. It is often this grounding that allows us to break free and invent new futures, or do wild and wacky things ...

"The only Zen you find on the tops of mountains is the Zen you bring up there'
Robert M. Pirsig

HOMES FOR THE FUTURE …

Where we come from determines many of our attitudes and responses in later life. This is not airy fairy psycho-babble; it is logical to suppose that if in our formative years we were responded to in a particular way, it would in some way influence our behaviour.

For example, children who have grown up in an insecure environment, unsure of how their parents will respond to them, are likely to develop behaviours that will get the best reactions from their parents and keep them 'approved of'.

Sometimes, this behaviour gets repeated in later life and the individual comes to believe that people's continuing approval of them is based on not being their authentic self, but upon being what other people expect them to be. Confidence that one is of value and significant as a unique individual is one of the most precious possessions that a person can have.

People who feel that they have to be compliant to the extent of denying their true nature or desires, are bound to remain dependent on external sources to maintain self-esteem. This renders them totally dependent on others and unable to grow or even get excited by what they do. It also makes them very vulnerable to the misfortunes of life which we all have to endure, for example, failure in an examination or job, rejection by a friend or lover, or loss of any kind. This last factor becomes acutely important in terms of **dealing with change.** These events make us all resentful or unhappy or both, but in the case of those with little or no self-esteem, it can be devastating, to the point where denial is a much safer option. Clearly this would render inventing their own future out of the question.

'In an era of increasing returns, we are better off wiring everybody, especially the poor. Philanthropy today is even more self-advantageous than it was in an industrial economy.

'Human society is based on work. The change in our work ethic was a change to include leisure, not to exclude work. Tools were made to facilitate work and let us think more. As we thought more, we developed new tools that do much of the thinking for us. Now that the physical and cognitive planes are covered, the next domain of "the tool" should be the soul. And when the digital view fully snares the domain of the soul, a new blueprint for empathy will be the first thing to emerge'
Watts Wacker

the changing rooms

61

As a reality hacker, you will notice that those
who feel envious of others who
'do what they want' will often be derogatory about them.

Be prepared to see this for what it is ...

We need to take where we have come from into consideration when inventing future routes. We do have to look at our experiences in a different way, in order for things to be able to progress. It isn't like shutting a door on the past, which is never to be opened; it's more like putting the bags in a closet, so that we know where they are, we know they exist, and we know just how big they are. We can open the closet door, look at them and then close it. They will always be there, whether we acknowledge them or not. It seems far more productive to use the experiences as perspectives and learning, rather than negative 'baggage'.

'The significant problems that we face cannot be solved by the same level of thinking we were at when we created them'
Albert Einstein

WE NEED TO MOVE ON WITH
HOME IN OUR HEARTS ...

The secret of understanding what anything means to us is dependent on how we have connected it to all the other things we know or have known. So there is no one 'real meaning' of anything, as it cannot exist in isolation. Something with just one meaning is one dimensional and has very little potential for development, as it can only lead us down one track. It is hard to conceive that with all the influences we have in our lives, that there could be only one meaning, one route, one path.

'Time present and time past
Are both perhaps present in time future,
And time future contained in time past'
T.S. Eliot, *Burnt Norton*

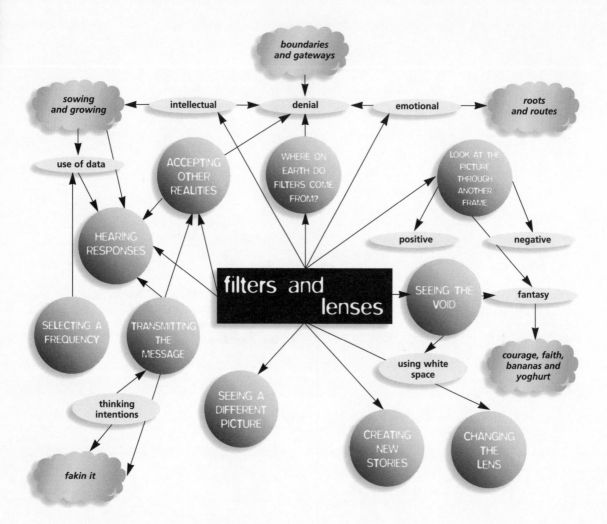

filters and lenses

How do we make sense or nonsense of everything we see?

How **does** the reality hacker view the world?

Our normal ways of thinking and speaking about reality are woefully inadequate for coping with our present circumstances, let alone inventing our futures. We develop filters and frames as a kind of shorthand for us to be able to manage and know what to expect in our worlds. The filters and frames come from experiences and expectations, and clearly inventing a future will depend on what we see through our own lenses.

How we express or make it happen is dependent on our filters of language and understanding. The frames consist of things like attitudes towards people, towards futures, towards the way the world works. The frames contain expectations, not certainties. They are guidelines as to what we can expect, based on what we have experienced so far. The frames are dynamic, dependent on our experiences and what we allow to develop and change. When they become static, we become unable to understand or hack either our own or others' realities. We tend not to 'discover' truth, but construct social realities.

Reality hackers need to be able to see the filters and lenses for what they are, and know what they are seeing, feeling and hearing.

They need to know when they are distorting reality and how to change the filters.

WHERE ON EARTH DO THE FILTERS COME FROM ?

There is an old adage that says that personnel people make up their minds about the people they are interviewing within the first five minutes of the interview, and then spend the rest of the interview proving this impression. Well, my guess would be that it isn't five minutes, but probably nearer twelve seconds.

We carry around in the back of our minds years and years of conditioning and judgements that we are not consciously aware of. If we walk into a pub or a party, we would find ourselves very quickly making decisions about who 'looks interesting', for the most spurious of reasons, such as they are wearing white towelling socks.

Often, we see what that sight reminds us of. The moment we sense a person, we connect visual clues about them to clues about others we have known, often imbuing them with the same characteristics as the other people. Not only do we imbue them with characteristics of others, but also the feelings we have had for the other person(s).

Even in the language we use, we evoke memories of the other's speech and the memories that they in turn may invoke. If a manager talks to his team in a very paternalistic way, that may bring up memories for the team members of their parents, and move them to respond to their manager in a similar way to how they responded to their parents.

Sue worked for a family organisation. She had worked there since she left university and was at the top end of middle management, in a very responsible job. She was highly rated by everyone, both internally and externally. She was promoted into another department with a new manager. Things went very quickly down hill.

She went from being calm, organised and cheery to aggressive, reticent and moody. Her personnel director tried to find out what the issues were, but was pushed away. Things came to a head at a presentation to a client, when she lost her temper with her manager and stormed out.

Having lost face, she went to the personnel manager with her resignation.

The personnel manager persisted this time, and got her to talk. She said she could not cope with the way she was told what to do by her new manager. She felt untrusted and that she could do nothing right but was incapable of talking to talk to him about it. The language she was using sounded very childlike to her personnel manager, and this was untypical of her.

After some sensitive questioning, Sue admitted that her manager reminded her of her father. Every time the manager had questioned her, she felt she was being interrogated by her father. Her child filters came into play, and suddenly she had found herself responding in exactly the same way she had in her youth. She began using words she had not used since adolescence. She expected trouble from him, and of course perceived all interaction as a potential battle.

She was horrified that someone was able to stir such old feelings to the extent that she was completely unaware of her behaviour, just of her extreme frustration.

Once she had talked it through, she tried to examine whether her filters had been fooled. She came to the conclusion that there were definitely similarities in behaviour that had aroused her child filters, but she was operating in her child's reality, not her current one.

It took some time for her to accept it all, but she eventually regained the confidence of her current reality, and was able to hack onward, and develop a true relationship with the manager.

These biases and filters are not things that we can, or even should,

get rid of.

We *do* need to be aware that they exist.

Iin their worst moments they will not only discolour what our

reality is, but also inhibit our ability to freely invent our future.

We talk about how we can read people like a book. Some people are a brochure or a pamphlet … they speak in sound bites, and we may even be inspired while we listen to them. Sometime later we may find ourselves suffering from MSG overdose — what did I really eat, and why am I still hungry?

What was it they really said, and why did my filters let it go? To know ourselves well enough to invent our future, we need the full version of the book, not an abridged copy, or the advertising blurb.

FILTERING IS ABOUT THE WAY WE FRAME THINGS

Do we frame things from a positive or negative point of view?

Do I describe what I don't want to do as opposed to what I want to do?

Some of us find it hard to frame our lives from the 'I want to do' position. British culture, for instance, has a filter of class that runs through most of our thoughts and actions. It is impossible to escape it, since if we have grown up in Britain, then we will have experienced it everywhere in our lives, from school to where we shop.

Knowing our place, sticking to it and conforming are key to being approved of in British society. What gets rewarded is the 'right' behaviour. Be a good girl, don't ask too many questions; children should be seen and not heard …

This is in direct contrast to American society, where you get rewarded not for adapting your behaviour, but for being successful, no matter how. The American myth goes that any person can grow up to be President. It doesn't matter whether it is really true or not if the myth is strong enough. That kind of cultural filter gives people the permission to try anything in pursuit of success. They tend to take more risks as the potential payoff is so high …

We need to bear this in mind when we consider our approach to problem solving.

When we speak of problem solving or indeed problem definition, we often say we will let the information speak for itself. That in itself is an interesting statement.

> **Everybody has their own information filter**
> **which allows them to both take in and view**
> **information as 'true'. Therefore each interested**
> **individual in a discussion will have a take on 'the truth' …**

> **(… which is certainly out there —**
> **it's just a question of whether we are**
> **free enough to know it or see it).**

'Animals studied by Americans rush about frantically, with an incredible display of hustle and pep, and at last achieve the desired result by chance. Animals observed by Germans sit still and think, and at last evolve the solution out of their inner consciousness.'
Bertrand Russell

Our perception of objectivity is bound by the interests of the perceiver, which in turn is shaped by our socio-cultural, emotional and intellectual restraints or lenses. Our memories are not immutable tape recorders. We remember combinations of images, and these combinations occur to us depending on what the trigger for memory has been. This makes them unreliable and often jumbled, unless we have made a special effort to keep them in the right order, as a trained observer, like a football referee, might do.

But as a television instant replay can show, even trained observers can get it wrong.

'History is what you remember, and if you don't think it's being revised all the time, you haven't paid enough attention to your own memory. When you remember something, you don't remember the thing itself — you just remember the last time you remembered it'
John Barlow

Our brains may record images and sounds,

but they are overlaid

with filters

and lenses ...

LOOK AT THE PICTURE THROUGH ANOTHER FRAME ...

Reality hacking demands the ability to function like a photographer. We need to know:

when to use which filters ...

> **when to take them off ...**

>> **when to use which lens ...**

>>> **and when to shoot from different angles.**

What kind of filters do we have?

What lenses do we use?

Aviva Sklan, an artist, explained that when she was learning to draw, and wasn't quite sure how to commit an object to paper, that she would look at the space around it, and that would enable her to see the object for how it filled that space.

Maybe it would help us if we could see the outline of a situation, rather than look at the detail, and see the space it occupies. Maybe that would help us get the perspective we need to be able to deal with it.

How do our own experiences fit into the BIGGER PICTURE?

How do we 'fit into the space'?

The outcome we get from an interaction depends

on the kinds of expectations we have.

The kinds of frames we use to solve the

problem, will depend on

which expectations need changing.

There is no combination of lens and filter that will be right for every shot. We have to look at what kind of picture we want to achieve, and then figure out what is necessary from there. Without that focus, we might end up using the wrong filters, but we are certainly unlikely to get what we want, as we never decided what that was in the first place.

There are many who will not want to consider frames, lenses and filters; this might lead them into questioning who they are, perhaps in a fundamental way. Our filters and lenses are there ... we need to see them for what they are. If we can't do that, we have no hope of changing them in order to look at the future. Some people memorise the lenses, and know their names but don't actually use them from the heart.

TRANSMITTING THE MESSAGE ...

Understanding communication demands understanding the language, interpreting the words into meaning, inferring the speaker's intent, then transmuting meaning into action as a result of the interpretation. Quite a lot to consider, even in that sentence ...

Language is more than words and sentences.

Without language, truth is not possible.

By having language, however, lying is possible ...

Understanding what people say involves more than the words alone. We have to understand the actions that are part of the language. We have to understand how the language is being used, and what it is responsible for.

What must we look for in others?

How can we understand the intent behind the words?

How can we ensure our message has been received?

In other words, understanding people is a complex maze of working through filters, conditioning and situational knowledge. Some of our motives are current, some come from the past.

KNOWLEDGE CAN BECOME ITS OWN FILTER ...

Everyday phrases reflect our way of looking at the world. For example, how often do we use the phrase, 'the thing is ...'? We have a tendency to objectify our world; make the issues we are considering objects, almost as a way of controlling them. 'Things' are rarely *actual* things, when we use that phrase: more often they are feelings or thoughts.

We are more responsive to things than people, and expect so much of objects.

Our indignation swells when change in objects fails to bring about a promised improvement. At work, when something goes well, we are more likely to say 'great system' than 'great user'.

One of the problems with objectifying feelings or thoughts is that we reach a conclusion about them before we have had time to reflect on their nature; they have become an entity before they were fully formed. This kind of premature conclusion acts as both a defence and boundary.

'Linguistic theory is concerned primarily with an ideal speaker-listener, in a completely homogenous speech-community, who knows its language perfectly and is unaffected by such grammatically irrelevant conditions as memory limitations, distractions, shifts of attention and interest, and errors (random or characteristic) in applying this knowledge of the language to actual performance'
Noam Chomsky

the changing rooms

SEEING THE VOID ...

Buddhists believe in the 'void', but they believe the void, or space, is always full. Western culture, designed around objects, makes it hard to see space. It is this space that enables us to see what might be rather than just what is.

courage, faith, bananas and yoghurt

One of our filters is a discomfort with silence, another form of space.

'THINGS' ONLY EXIST BY VIRTUE OF THE SPACE AROUND THEM ...

The use of space and intervals, and the conviction that the elements omitted from a work of art are as much a part of that work as those included has been a speciality of the East for centuries.

In music, the Western classical tradition emphasises the continuous, connected worlds of melody and harmony, while the East was concerned with the role of silence. As certain Western ideas have migrated East, so certain Eastern ideas have begun to migrate West: for example, Stravinsky and Count Basie both incorporated in their work an awareness of fragmentation and intervals.

What Westerners often refer to in a somewhat derogatory fashion as the inscrutability of the East, is quite often the ability to live with and move within silences. Certainly living with ambiguity involves the ability to navigate silence and space ...

'Don't fence me in'
Cole Porter

HEARING RESPONSES ...

When we listen to people, what we hear are a bunch of words strung together: we are never completely certain of the meaning and intent behind the words ... either our own or others. (Count the number of times you say, or you hear others say, 'I didn't mean that' or 'you don't understand me'.)

Most of our communications are imperfect. We usually know in our heads what we want to say and what we mean, but it doesn't always come out that way. This may have nothing to do with our oratorical abilities, but more with the conscious and unconscious filters at work.

Sometimes we think we know what we mean ...

... and think we have said it.

THE OTHER PERSON'S RESPONSE IS THE ONLY MEANS WE HAVE OF DETERMINING WHETHER WE HAVE GOT OUR MESSAGE ACROSS.

Yet we pay less attention to their response than we do to formulating what we want or need to say next.

On those rare occasions when we do actually listen to someone else, we have to work out what it is that they mean by what they said, without knowing what is going on inside their heads. Many clues come from the non-verbal communications that accompany the spoken word, and the kind of words people say, but if we are too busy thinking about our message, we miss them.

We need to become more aware of what is *not* being said rather than just what is spoken — of the space around the words.

Can we make room for s p a c e ?

Can we hear silence?

ACCEPTING OTHER REALITIES ...

We are all very talented at blocking out the things we don't want to hear, sometimes subtly, sometimes less subtly.

Our filters are at work.

We build our personal realities in our minds. When we feel we cannot 'connect' with another person, often this is because our 'realities' differ. Does this mean that any person's reality is right or wrong? Or better or worse than another's?

Reality hackers understand and respond to different realities, both in ourselves and in others. Accepting the validity of another 'reality' is hard to do because of where we have come from. Conflicting realities are painful, but not death inducing.

Sometimes we want to convey our personal mental model or construct to someone else: sometimes it is too fragile to share and so, scared of rejection, or of looking stupid, we mask it. We mask or filter in many ways:

by using long sentences and big words

by obscure metaphors

by using humour

... the list goes on ...

Some people need time and space to think it out; others need time and space to talk it out.

Sara and Jonathan were two very different characters, who nobody would have put together in a relationship. She was all heart and feeling, he found it difficult to talk about himself and what he did with any honesty. She was compulsively honest.

They had tremendous affection for each other, but both of them needed something the other couldn't give. They talked and talked about it, but could not really accept each other's filters and lenses.

Their different lenses and filters sparked off destructive behaviour in each other that compounded their unhappiness. They could not break the pattern until they accepted each other's frame, and realised that allowing each other to see things differently was not an obstacle to their relationship, but a key part of it.

They were different but, instead of valuing the difference, they allowed it to come between them.

Sara needed to talk it out, Jonathan needed to think it out. They were both trying to hack a different reality.

It took an enforced spell apart – in which she was able to talk it out, and he was allowed to think it out – for them to be able to see the lenses. Understanding this helped them to grasp and hack their own realities, rather than a fantasy for their relationship ...

It does take time, acceptance and trust; the jury is still out ...

Sometimes we need space, when what we *think* we need is resolution. When we are desperate for answers or a way out of the pain we are feeling, we think we will get it by finding 'an answer'. What we often need is the time to reflect, and permission to know that that is all right. Some of us need the space to think it out ourselves, some of us need someone to talk it out to. Understanding those lenses for ourselves is an essential part of inventing our future.

SELECTING A FREQUENCY ...

We have a need to categorise before we have the context in which we are categorising. In nouveau technology speak, do we need a taxonomy or a search engine?

Roughly translated, that means do we need to index, specify and classify, or define an approach to accessing information?

Once we have the information, we need to understand what to do with it, and also how we will find it at a later date. Quite often it is not our memory that has failed, but rather our retrieval system. Our memory records what we have experienced, but we are not always able to access the information at a later date, thereby rendering the information useless.

One way of arranging the information is by using what John Spence described as a memory palace. In this process, we develop in our minds a schematic of a building, a palace (because it would have to be a large building), and where in that building we have stored the information. By doing this we are able to bring up in our minds a picture of where the rooms are, the walkways from one room to another, which rooms are full or empty and so on.

Even if we can develop this way of 'seeing' our minds, we also need to understand that memories and information are stored everywhere. They are better perceived as evoked, rather than found. The keys to the room in the palace might be a picture, a person, or a song ...

What we are able to access acts as a filter in itself.

If we can only access half a story, then we will base our next steps on half a story, and we start to consider solutions based on missing information.

Preparing solutions in advance also stops us reading other people's signals, and our own. We become fixated on carrying out the solution rather than checking to see whether it is appropriate. This makes the level of panic even greater when we finally realise that it hasn't worked.

Reality hacking implies an ability to transcend conditioned filters, in order to respond to the here and now. That means not trying to control the future, but seeing what is happening in front of us.

the changing rooms

85

One way of observing our impact on others is to carry on behaving as we normally do, but pay very close attention to the reactions of people when we say what we do or describe our work or home. Many 'self-development programmes' focus on changing yourself … that is very hard to do when we are not clear about how other people see us. Actually being able to see the effect we have on others is far more likely to motivate us to change the way we behave than reading about how other people perceive we 'should' be.

'If you tug on any piece of the universe, you'll find that everything else is attached to it'
John Muir

Filtering often means that a perception about certain words or behaviours gets logged in our minds, it becomes static, and not of the moment when it was spoken. When we hear the word 'vision', for example, some people will interpret it as some ghastly idea dreamt up by senior executives which 'defines' what they want to do with their organisation. For others it might mean a religious experience.

The way we have framed that word will determine how we respond to it.

If we are become sophisticated reality hackers, we need to be able to get past our personal constructs and experience to know what we or another person wishes to convey by their use of the words.

We connect values to words, and thereby give ourselves permission to label them good or bad. Words like **courage** and **faith** sound charismatic and airy fairy. We perceive them as nice to have rather than crucial to our lives. **Vision literally means being able to see and feel a future** ... what an incredible act to be able to perform. It should not be something committed to paper, but a picture that people carry inside of them, one that they can connect to and live with.

courage, faith, bananas and yoghurt

When we talk about people 'buying in' to solutions, what actually happens is that they can see what we can see and feel what we can feel when we paint the picture.

This is reality communication.

Dell Hymes suggests an acronym, **SPEAKING**, which supplies ideas for the kind of framework we need to be considering when speaking ...

Setting

Participants

Ends they are striving for

acts they are engaged in

Key or tone in which the talking is being done **I**nstruments or tools to get the job done **N**orms that apply to the situation **g**enre of talk they are engaged in

Some of the issues feel as though they have been put in to make the word up but, by and large, **SPEAKING** makes a useful analytical planning tool, and might help consider some of the potential dynamics at work. It does miss the intuitive heart and soul of an interaction, but makes us pay attention to some of the key filters. Language does have a tendency to reinforce cultural acceptability, that is, if we use the 'right' words we become acceptable to the person we are speaking to.

This means we have to be continuously aware, at either a conscious or subconscious level, of people's different frames of reference in order to be 'acceptable' to them.

'What a waste it is to lose one's mind, or not to have a mind is very wasteful. How true that is'
Dan Quayle

CHANGING THE LENS ...

In order to hack reality, we have to be able to see it.

Learning to perceive and evaluate information, and then reacting appropriately raises all the threats thrown up by not using traditional methods of perception. It leads us to the questions 'How will I know the truth?' and 'What can I believe in with certainty?'.

A recurrent theme of this book is that that certainty does not exist in our world, and acceptance of that is essential to reality hacking.

'(All) thinking is metaphorical, except mathematical thinking ... What I am pointing out is that unless you are at home in the metaphor, unless you have had your proper poetical education in the metaphor, you are not safe anywhere. Because you are not at ease with figurative values, you don't know the metaphor in its strength and its weaknesses. You don't know how far you may expect to ride it and when it may break down with you. You are not safe in science; you are not safe in history ...

'All metaphor breaks down somewhere. That is the beauty of it. it is touch and go with the metaphor, and until you've lived with it long enough you don't know when it is going'

Robert Frost

WE NEED **TO** DEVELOP WAYS OF DEALING WITH INFORMATION **THAT** ALLOW FOR UNCERTAINTY, AND ARE NOT ROOTED IN SOMEONE ELSE'S PERCEIVED CERTAINTY

One way we do this already without thinking, is by using metaphors. When we look at a concept that is important to us, but is difficult to grasp, like feelings, time etc., we instinctively use metaphors to allow us to grasp something which otherwise would seem ungraspable. Metaphors can be a means to define boundaries and ease re-framing of issues or actions. They can change the atmosphere in which issues are discussed, and help adjust expectations.

When reinventing our future, we need to think about how we can use and re-work metaphors to capture our vision of the future. Changing the dominant metaphor in our lives might be a powerful way of re-perceiving our issues and/or opportunities, and changing the lens. For example, if you currently see yourself as a hamster on a treadmill, how would you like to see yourself?

SEEING A DIFFERENT PICTURE ...

Living in today's changeable climate means the ability to change lenses very quickly.

As we have seen, accepting other people's reality in relation to our own is very important. Being able to change the lens is the next step.

> *Janine is a Frenchwoman who has been living in England with Ian, her English husband, for the last two years. When they met and were both living and working together in Paris, they both shared the same metaphors for living: they had interesting and absorbing jobs, a need for recognition and a need to belong. When they moved to England because of Ian's job, they still shared the same love of food, music and the cinema. However, her framing of her life, her metaphors, were still back in Paris.*
>
> *She saw things in the same way she had seen them then; particularly because she had her family, who were very important to her, very close by. As time wore on, Ian's comfort with his home territory grew, almost in direct proportion to Janine's discomfort. Her metaphors, in her insecurity, had become stronger as she sought relief in old visions. She felt very much an outsider. She was not in close proximity to her family, her work had not materialised in the way she had hoped, and she did not feel part of anything.*
>
> *She found herself unable to discuss things with Ian, as she did not want to disturb his apparent happiness. The more difficulty she had speaking about herself, the stronger the old metaphors grew, and her self-perceived out-of placeness in England became greater.*
>
> *She had not settled in a job, and they were living in a friend's flat. She had no tangible vision of place, and the only picture of home was from Paris.*

It was not until she returned to her family for a short holiday that her displacement became so apparent that she could not hide it from Ian any longer.

They then both suffered the great pain of not knowing what to do. In their separate frames, they had positioned each other as only able to live in certain physical circumstances, and found it very hard to face up to the fact that neither one of them was able to cope with not having their needs met.

*If the positions were reversed, the dynamic would have been exactly the same: one partner out of sync with the other's metaphor of life. Inventing their future has required them to invent a metaphor for the life they want to lead **together**, regardless of place or old history. They both have pasts and roots, but hacking their future reality means deciding how they want to be together, now and in the future.*

It is actually much easier to try to decide that by looking at the past, but they have to develop new filters and lenses to cope with their current reality, not ones that were created for them.

In the age of globalism we have entered, we will find ourselves constantly engaging other people's filters. Both individuals and organisations who want to hack the future need to be able not only to accept the difference, but be able to adjust the lenses appropriately.

So what metaphors might serve reality hackers?

Well, reality hacking itself is one: it conjures up many pictures of technology and newness, and also making your way through something. Metaphors such as cultivate, seed, harvest, potential, ebb and flow, both/and, are all pictures of more fluid boundaries.

In everyday things are embedded the unusual; the unpredictable and the unique always accompany the expected and reliable. If we are looking at transformation, we can see how we can use the flower metaphor: from bud to bloom, to fruit, to decay, to seed …

HOW ABOUT COURAGE, FAITH, BANANAS AND YOGHURT … ?

Listen to your own metaphors and those around you — how many are sport or, more often, war related?

Reality hackers don't see the world that way:

War metaphors

winner/loser

fixed

beginning/ending

contradiction

Reality hackers' metaphors

collaborator

continuous

cyclicity

counterpoint

Add to this all the learning metaphors — **discovery, exploration, adventure, insight, vulnerability, error** — and you begin to approach the reality hackers' vocabulary ...

CREATING NEW STORIES ...

To re-frame our present, past and future we often use 'stories'. Most of our current stories are in the form of technical reports rich in theory and data, that imply authority and objectivity. However, the stories which have the most impact on us, particularly at gut level, are those that elicit feelings at that gut level; that is feelings of fear, hope etc.

We need to be able to move from creating myths of uncertainty, to myths which embrace uncertainty. If we are so certain of things, then we have nothing to learn. Yes, it's that river in Egypt again ... denial. Our facts are always the product of selective perceptions and beliefs, and these are always underpinned by emotions. If we focus only on 'facts', we are denying what is behind them.

NATURAL DISRUPTIONS TO OUR WAY OF LIFE ARE HERE TO STAY

We invented language without any understanding of what lay beneath it. If we look at other inventions, they all get upgraded or adapted as a result of scientific development – we used to write letters. Look at the language we use now: yes, it's changed, but have we adapted?

Once we understand our filters and lenses, and the way we communicate and receive, we can greatly increase our ability to adapt and perform in the environment around us.

Reality hackers cannot predict the future, because that would just be more spurious data, but they try to anticipate what might be.

When we learn to do that without fear, we can consider options. It even allows us to grow ideas in the event of a crisis. We are back to asking the right questions as opposed to finding the right answers, and learning how to adapt and find new lenses, particularly as the questions keep changing ...

'My face in thine eye,
thine in mine appears,
and true plain hearts
in the faces rest.'
John Donne

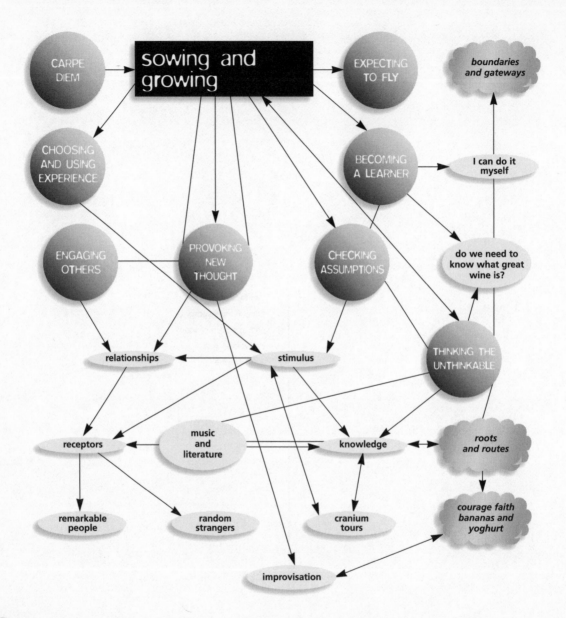

sowing and growing

'All organisms with complex nervous systems are faced with the moment by moment question that is posed by life: What shall I do next?'
Sue Savage Rumaugh and **Roger Lewin**, 1994

The gentle art of growing is a complex process and for that reason this section may initially read differently. Don't give up — the difference is all.

Where do I go from here?

the life question . . .

This is where reality hackers start to consider what their future might look like, and what they might need to get there. We can invent a future with no thought as to how it might come to pass, but reality hacking is about making a future real.

We endlessly create and recreate ourselves. Our minds are a fluctuating view of how we combine our inner and outer worlds. This creation is partly under our control and partly hidden from our reflections. At night when we sleep it is almost totally out of control. We do so much without 'thinking', and yet we insist on logic and order as part of a growth process. We need to know how seeds get planted, nurtured and can maintain sustainable growth.

Sowing and Growing is about understanding where the growth comes from, what it looks like, and what it will take for us to do it.

We have

many stimuli on offer

both from inside ourselves

and outside.

Capitalising on them

and the opportunities

they present

is the journey

of the reality hacker.

Reality hacking depends on engagement: we need to know *ourselves* before we can believe and invent; without engagement we cannot embrace change or growth in any form. Engagement is not about intellectual courage, it is about feeling and understanding ourselves, our perspective, and our values.

EXPECTING TO FLY ...

Most organisations measure achievement by upward improvement only; in sales, profits and careers. If you don't want to progress up the organisation you are perceived as a low achiever. Personal growth is framed by speed of promotion.

But promotion is not growth, it is opportunity. It is rarely the only way to grow and it indeed can impede 'maturation'. What passes for growth is often enlargement of status and position. Learning is about awareness, not necessarily movement.

GROWTH IN TERMS OF CONSTANT ONWARDS AND UPWARDS, WHICH IS HOW MANY OF US PERCEIVE IT, IS NOT NECESSARILY WHAT WE SHOULD BE WISHING FOR

We tend to be obsessive about growth, whether it is related to personal, economic or social issues. How can we take it into our hearts without first asking what growth *really* means, for what, for whom and for how long?

All the metaphors for our lives see growth as upward, but most plants and the tallest trees send down roots as well as reaching towards the light.

roots and routes

Of course, where we come from and our need and desire to grow comes from our roots. Where we come from determines how we perceive the way forward.

Growth is not necessarily all about newness: at a deeper level it is also about awareness and acceptance of what already exists; a level of maturity. Any organism has a growth cycle which includes maturation. We talk about *physical* maturation, yet avoid *psychological* maturation …

… so how can we learn
what growing means to us?

Some of our disaffection with life stems from an incongruence between our expectations, subconscious aspirations and what actually happens. In other words, we build up a picture in our heads of how something or someone will 'be'.

EVEN THE ACT OF PREDICTION MAKES US FEEL IN CONTROL AND POWERFUL

However, when we have a day which is filled with unpredictability, traffic jams, and conflicting demands, we are left frustrated by the mismatch between what we expected and what actually happened. William Calvin calls this 'environmental incoherence', and suggests the cure for it is to scale down the number of challenges you set for yourself to a level where you will be right at least half the time. Sometimes after a day of unpredictability we take refuge in rituals, music that we are familiar with, or 'mindless' television or films, where we *know* what will happen next ... This seems to make us feel better, more in control of our world.

Sometimes our perceptions can be restricted to what we are anticipating or expecting to happen, but with some slight modifications. We seem to only notice something if we are looking for it, or if someone points it out to us.

'We need a long life to get on our feet'
James Hillman

Instead of talking and knowing,

we might be better prepared for reality,

and increase our ability to hack it,

if we did more observing and noticing.

It is hard consciously to take in everything we see in a room, but we usually notice if something has changed.

How can we see more?

Close your eyes now and try to visualise the room you are in. Can you describe the objects in it? What colours are they?

Keep your eyes closed and try to visualise the last time you saw the people you work with.

Can you remember what they were wearing, what they said or what they were doing?

Even when we do notice, sometimes we choose to ignore it. It is so out of step with what we expected or wanted that we choose not to acknowledge it.

Learning is the result of recognising and USING the difference between what you expected and what actually happens.

Recognition of self, what self is and what self needs and wants, is key to growth.

'A man at the dinner table dipped his hands in the mayonnaise and then ran them through his hair. When his neighbour looked astonished, he said "I'm so sorry. I thought it was spinach"'
Sigmund Freud

What do we see
when we look in the mirror?

Is it what we want to see or what there is?

How do we know what it is we want to see?

How much of what we see is governed by what we think we ought to be seeing?

What does growth mean for me?

These kinds of questions, while important to answer if we wish to invent our futures, are enough to send us scurrying into panic. As the character Marcy in the Peanuts cartoon is reported to have said: 'Some questions make your teeth hurt, your eyes stream and ears ache ...' We are convinced we must come up with an instant answer, or we jump to a conclusion about ourselves so that at least we have something.

Suggestibility and stress increase our

propensity and need

to jump to conclusions.

When we are frightened in

the broadest sense of the word,

our need for instant explanation

may make us leap

to totally irrational conclusions.

Even simple fears like hearing noises in an empty house can lead us to explanations that range from a dripping tap to worries that we have Alzheimer's disease, depending on our panic levels. We dream frightening and highly unlikely scenarios. If they are the *only* explanations we come up with, we can make ourselves extremely unhappy.

Again our need for action often results in premature closure. We either stop looking around, or pick on something that gives us instant gratification. Sometimes we see things that are not really there.

The dynamics of these situations develop false realities, and encourage suspicion and mistrust. Not surprisingly these factors inhibit rather than encourage growth.

CHECKING ASSUMPTIONS ...

How do we deal with all the data that we amass?

How do we make sense of the jumble that is us?

There does seem to be a pattern in the way we collect, store and recall information. We experience situations, make observations and, depending on our state of mind at the time, draw conclusions about individuals and events.

Having drawn these conclusions we use those data the next time we find ourselves in a similar situation. The inferences we draw therefore become 'true' in our heads, and colour our subsequent thinking. If we do not check our understanding, we will not be dealing with a reality, but an assumption. Dealing merely with assumptions and inferences will result in fantasy hacking, or at least hacking the wrong reality.

So how do we check ourselves out?

FIRST OF ALL WE HAVE
TO GIVE OURSELVES PERMISSION
TO ASK THE QUESTIONS; TO BE
ALLOWED TO CHECK

We don't ask enough questions. We are in too much of a hurry to get to resolution, terrified that if we stop and reflect or ask ourselves or others questions it will somehow inhibit our ability to act and resolve the issue. We find it hard to consider reflection and questioning as action …

We need to be a little careful here; this is not about putting off action, but about checking that our sensors have picked up accurate information on which to base our thoughts and subsequent actions.

Here engagement comes to the fore ...

How do we check out perceptions of self and others?

We need to be able to both engage and disengage.

We need to be able to pick up and absorb new and/or novel behaviours, to perceive, think and act differently.

IF WE BEHAVE AS WE ALWAYS BEHAVED, THEN WE GET WHAT WE ALWAYS GOT...

BECOMING A LEARNER ...

Inventing our future necessitates some feeling of newness, even if it is just a new set of lenses for looking at the world. How we get these innovations into our lives depends on our personal characteristics and our need and desire to learn.

Kurt Lewin and his followers suggest that you cannot know an institution until you try to change it, and you cannot change it without reflecting on its purpose. This not only applies to organisations but to the general pursuit of individual reality hacking.

> **We never really know our full potential**
> **until we try and grow, and we cannot do that**
> **without first considering what we are about.**

Don Michael wrote in 1983 that we can seldom *change* things from A to B, since we do not always know what it is we are changing, or what we want to change to. B, by definition, cannot be a known totality. For this reason, whatever we do is by way of *affecting* a situation, instead of changing it.

This way of looking at things may help us avoid some of the frustration and despair that results from trying to control change, in a world where everything is connected to everything else.

Becoming a learner is not only a difficult challenge to take up, but is also a road that is difficult to stay on. When we think about learning, we usually think about a well-defined end or the search for a single solution to a single problem.

Learning in order to grow demands continuous questioning. Don Michael suggests four phases:

1. Learning to re-perceive or reinterpret a situation

2. Learning to apply the re-perception to formulate policy or action

3. Learning how to implement the policies or actions

4. Learning to keep the first three open to continual revision

Learning is also about adjusting to an environment where we are no longer behaving as people expect. In fact, we are less likely to learn if we feel that it will in some way alienate us. We are attracted by being ourselves, inventing our own futures, being an individual; but we are also terrified of not being accepted. Although the results of new learning and growth may eventually meet our needs and grow us as individuals, the act of learning seems to compound our sense of vulnerability. Maybe it is this exact experience of touching vulnerability, and still remaining whole, that actually allows us to grow.

During periods of change there have to be periods of disruption, confusion and changing circumstances.

the changing rooms

During times of change we need to create nurturing environments that support our learning and vulnerability.

GROWTH IS LEARNING

LEARNING DEPENDS ON RISK

We can only adjust to a world of diversity by being aware of the connectivity and interdependencies that exist in our new world.

CHOOSING AND USING EXPERIENCE ...

So where do we get our
learning from?

The interesting thing is that we can take ourselves to the water, but we don't necessarily drink even though at one level we want to. We can be with wildly stimulating people, or engaged in extremely demanding sport, but these situations will not open up our future if we have incongruent or unachievable expectations of them.

This in turn takes us back to the intent we had when we took up the new pursuit ...

... what were we expecting
to happen?

We put so much activity into changing external things in our lives.

We look for better jobs, better homes, better husbands and wives, better ski tips.

Although we can alter our lives by changing our environments, most significant changes occur when we find effective ways to change our inner landscape, because that is the environment we always have with us.

Experiencing is our fundamental activity, and so the quality of our lives depends on the quality of our experience. That in turn depends on our state of mind. If our lives are not as satisfying as they might be, is that the fault of our current circumstances or of our inability to appreciate them?

Is the true cause of discontent internal or external?

Are many of our external conflicts the result of our internal unrest?

BEFORE WE LOOK OUTSIDE FOR DEVELOPMENT SOURCES, WE NEED TO CHECK INSIDE ...

Sometimes it takes a traumatic life event to allow us to appreciate and experience the here and now: to appreciate what both we and life have to offer, and take it rather than judge it ...

'The only Zen you experience at the tops of mountains is the Zen you bring'
– Robert M. Pirsig

Learning and growing through outside stimuli is part of our future, but not the answer.

Something which confronts us every day is our fixation with what we are told is the 'information age'. The idea being sold to us is that somehow, having access to lots of information, particularly via the Internet, will change our lives. There it is again; something happening outside of us will change our lives. Why don't *we* have a go?

Changing our lives through information can only happen if we know what information we need and why we want it. Logically, how could just having truckloads of information change our lives? It doesn't make any sense.

Let's take Ben Long's theory of technology evolution:

Neanderthal man had a huge brain, much larger than ours. However, it was not stuffed with art, reason or religion, because he didn't have any. Apparently, the theory goes that he did not need any reason or logic because the brain was so big it remembered everything.

Because it remembered everything, it didn't need to know how to transfer knowledge or use rationale to solve a problem.

'Thinking is more interesting than knowing, but less interesting than looking'
Goethe

This is how the information agers would have us be ...

Use the Web, its all there, tune in, surf on, log out, be there ...

... you don't have to think or learn.

This isn't really learning or even information, but stimulus, and should be regarded as such. It should be seen as an opening to help us to move on and grow, but not the answer or the way.

INFORMATION ITSELF IS NOT THE ANSWER

The danger is that an information glut will prevent us from going higher than knowledge-level thinking: that is, we take the information, but either have no use for it, or do not know how and where to apply it. We need to know the questions before we seek answers.

Having information so readily available, and portrayed as the answer to our problems, is more insidious than our old and still current education system, in which we are programmed to learn by rote, and are only 'allowed' to question at fixed points. This has got us into the habit of wanting either to be told what to do, or to have our actions validated by an authority figure.

The consequence of this for learning and our ability to grow is that we fix it in someone else's perspective. If we want to invent our future, we need to be more aware of what it is *we* are looking for, and **then** use the information to help draw the route-map. The information alone will not take us there, because it can't. It is, after all, only data without a context.

If we are looking at information gathering in order to gain knowledge to encourage growth, we need to be able to contextualise it, that is, be aware of what we expect to gain from it, and how we will use it once we have it. If we don't do this, there can be no growth, just accumulation of data. This doesn't mean, however, that we are only allowed to open ourselves to experiences which have focused outcomes. Some of our most inspired stimuli for growth are likely to have come from unexpected sources: a conversation in a pub, a chance meeting at a conference, a magazine article.

The aspiring reality hacker has at his or her disposal any number of known and yet-to-be-known stimuli, which have been experienced or described to them. The *Reality Hacker's Resource Guide* at the end of the book is one hacker's non-exhaustive collection. What would be in your resource guide? Remember it is never finished — the hacker is forever open to new experiences.

We do need to be to be open to taking in unsolicited information, which, by its nature, is unlikely to have an obvious or immediate use.

filters and lenses

We need to be able to take on the information and know in which room in our memory palace we have stored it so that it can come to life, when appropriate, and be used to enrich experience, rather than being merely more information.

Sometimes what we seek is right there in front of us, and we just need to see it in a different way. The way we regard a piece of work we have to do is very dependent on our mood at the time. We can look at an article or book in one way and, two days later, because of an experience or mood, look at it completely differently. When we struggle to make sense of our reality, it sometimes helps to move right away from whatever is confusing us, or look at it again in or from another context.

When I was writing this book, towards the end, I was having trouble concentrating. I had been away from home to clear my mind and focus on what I wanted to write. That had worked extremely well, as my mind felt free of everything else and I was able to let my thoughts flow freely. When I returned home to finish the book, I was back in distracting circumstances; I was sitting at my 'work' desk, with my 'work' computer, surrounded by 'work' papers.

It took me a couple of disoriented days, and a comment from a friend to change the pattern. She said, 'go back to San Francisco if that's where you felt comfortable' …Well, that was not practical or affordable, but it made me consider the circumstances under which I had been able to grow. I abandoned the 'work' room, and took my portable computer, which had been away with me, into the kitchen and started work on the kitchen table, sometimes playing the same music I had been playing whilst away. Recreating the atmosphere worked, and I was able to regain the perspective I had had.

We often don't give ourselves the time to
think about the environments
that help us learn.

They won't always be the same.

Sometimes we overlook the obvious,
just because it is.

HACKING REALITY MEANS
KNOWING YOUR ENVIRONMENTS

THINKING THE UNTHINKABLE ...

Sometimes reality hacking also means *not knowing*.

Sometimes we have to put what we know out of our heads, and think about what we don't know. Turning our perspective on its head and thinking what we have not thought before, is a necessary technique for inventing futures. This may mean being in a completely different place or environment.

One of the fads of the nineties has been talking about thinking the unthinkable. Many recent pieces of legislation should have remained unthinkable or untaught, and may not necessarily come under the heading of innovative and/or risky thought. In March 1964, James Fulbright told the United States Senate: 'We must dare to think about unthinkable things because, when things become unthinkable, thinking stops and action becomes mindless.' It's hard to tell what he really meant by that, but perhaps he was suggesting that when no one ever challenges perceived wisdom, the point of action becomes lost.

However, parameters and definitions of what is unthinkable depend on an organisation's or individual's personal constructs. The proposition that Britain will drop out of the first division of world economies early in the next century to be replaced by China, India and Brazil seems more like a projection of the inevitable, but it is unthinkable to certain sections of the British establishment.

The unthinkable, whether personal or professional, is more often than not merely the unpalatable.

What would be unthinkable for us?

Is it unthinkable because it is unpalatable or because it is unknown, and therefore risky?

courage, faith, bananas and yoghurt

Growth is not just about the unthinkable or unpalatable …

Be careful what you wish for, you just might get it …

'In tests of convergent thinking there is almost always one conclusion or answer that is regarded as unique, and thinking is to be channelled or controlled in the direction of that answer … In divergent thinking, on the other hand, there is much searching about or going off in different directions. This is most obviously seen when there are no unique conclusions. Divergent thinking … is characterised … as being less goal bound. There is freedom to go off in different directions … Rejecting the old solution and striking out in some direction is necessary, and the resourceful organism will more probably succeed'
J.P. Guilford, 1959

PROVOKING NEW THOUGHT ...

Where do we get our learning experiences from?

When do we get insight that tells us we have a starting point for growth?

Identifying and creating opportunities and a nurturing environment requires a combination of both knowledge and foresight. Both of these words need definition.

We need to have enough knowledge to begin.

All plans have to have a starting point.

We also need to be able to improvise with what we've got.

'Discovery consists of seeing what everybody has seen and thinking what nobody has thought'
Albert Szent-Gyorgi

Improvisation is a combination of intuition and experience; you cannot improvise from nothing, you have to have something to improvise from and/or with. It is not about either what we can see or what might be. We need to look at the world as both/and rather than either/or. Either/or is a restrictive way of looking at the world and by its nature is limiting and demotivating. It prevents us from seeing the connectivity in the world which allows us to hack a total reality, rather than an isolated one.

KEEP YOUR MIND OPEN ...
... AT ALL TIMES

When do thoughts happen? Well, the answer is any time — our growth is dependent on our ability to recognise them as such. How many times have you 'slept on a problem' to have the answer clear as daylight in the daylight? Alternatively, how many times have you been so keen for closure and resolution that you have shut down thinking?

William Calvin suggests that the most frequent cause of premature closure in children is a short attention span. That is, they get bored and want an answer quickly, any answer. (Many of us continue this habit into adulthood ...)

In adulthood, it is usually our logic that brings us too soon to conclusions. When something fits, we stop looking at alternatives.

Sometimes, we are at an end of the process, but more often we have taken the line of least resistance, and certainly the first reasonable sounding option. Again this usually stems from our fear of not being in control, and the fear that we may not find any solution, so we go for the first one available. Sometimes it is not obvious what the alternative is, so we consider it best to go with something rather than nothing, or so we perceive.

'Children and adults don't have short attention spans: only bored children and adults do'
Ben Long

123

Quick solutions and systems can be the reality hacker's enemy.

They can keep us locked into solutions without knowing the problem we are solving. By its very nature, doing what you have always done will prevent growth. Frameworks do save us from having to evaluate everything from scratch, but strict adherence has its hazards.

'Convictions are more dangerous enemies of truth than lies'
Nietzsche

Even physics has had to give up determinism for fuzzy sets ...

Animals that stick to a routine, despite everything, get eaten. They have to adjust.

Dealing with inconsistency and the unthinkable is part of nature's evolutionary strategy, so why should it not be part of our micro-strategy?

Species that don't adapt don't survive.

Systems that cannot change with cultural need will break down.

If we are to invent futures that will excite us, we need to allow the excitement to brew in the thinking, not wait until the action ...

CARPE DIEM ...

Seizing the excitement and opportunity whenever we feel it, is the joy of the reality hacker.

The moment of learning is the climax of the excitement ...

Learning comes from knowledge acquisition, relationships and experiences. It is usually the relationship between the first thing and the second and third things that makes the development happen, and becomes a new stage in our growth. Seizing the time and/or opportunity is at the heart of reality hacking.

Sometimes we miss the opportunity for growth, or don't identify it as such. We have in the back of our minds that certain experiences are almost 'designated' growth or learning experiences: for example, if we go to a training workshop, or read a non-fiction book.

In many ways, our deepest learning comes from exposure to things other than the obvious. It may not even be knowledge acquisition; it may be insight.

It may be something a person says, a moment in a film, or during a walk. You know that moment, when you are least thinking about something, but suddenly everything becomes clear. Sometimes it happens just as we are falling off to sleep. Actually opening our minds to these small but significant moments is a major part of inventing futures. It is about getting in touch with the white space in our head.

roots and routes

Even experiencing and enjoying a thing of beauty, whether it's a movie, a picture or a landscape, the moment of realisation is so fast, and so transient. When we try and replay it, either through memory, or photographs, we are more conscious of it, and so experience it in a different way, and wonder why the feeling is not so strong.

filters and lenses

We need to justify, categorise and ground experiences or feelings, rather than just having them. This may have something to do with living in a Newtonian world, where everything has its own cause and effect. We get uncomfortable when we cannot identify one or the other or both. Reality hacking demands a suspension of that need.

In the more fluid environment of the last years of the twentieth century, there has been much talk of chaos theory and the application of quantum physics to everyday life. Even the idea that we search for a theory and solution tells us that we are still unprepared to go with the flow.

In quantum physics, if you know all the beginning circumstances and conditions, precisely, you can totally predict the final outcome, with certainty. What you cannot predict or prove, is what will happen in the middle. In other words, the total opposite of cause and effect: you don't know how things get from A to B, but they definitely do.

the changing rooms

Working in that space in the middle, and trusting what might happen, is one of the excitements of creating your own future. This is operating in the confusion room.

courage, faith, bananas and yoghurt

The continuing journey of the reality hacker is operating in and using the white space in between events.

what's here? …

Reality hacking is

about being able to see

the white spaces in life

and seizing the

opportunities

that lie in wait there.

The opportunity is not
necessarily delineated
explicitly, so we
have to look
beyond what is
obvious.

ENGAGING OTHERS ...

We can only deal with so much ambiguity.

When we are uncertain, we seek comfort in, amongst other things, religion, leaders, alcohol or technology. To cope with ambiguity we share our fears with others; it increases our capacity to learn and do.

courage, faith, bananas and yoghurt

We need to consider our relationships with others as gateways to learning.

'It is creative apperception more than anything else that makes the individual feel that life is worth living'
D.W. Winnicott

WHERE WE GET OUR
PLEASURE FROM IS THE VERY
KEY TO GROWING AND ENGAGING
WITH OURSELVES AND
OUR FUTURE ...

There is a myth that we only find fulfilment from interpersonal relationships. Indeed, much has been written about how having 'relationships' is the key to an individual's happiness. Many self-help books focus on this means of achieving happiness.

However, many 'interests', from speculating on the stock exchange, through rock climbing and pigeon fancying, play a greater part in the economy of human happiness than many allow. Enthusiastic gardeners may leave evidence of their passion which lasts for years, but nothing remains of an individual's passion for windmills or baseball. Yet we all know people whose lives have been enriched by their interests, whether or not their personal relationships were satisfactory.

129

Our expectation that satisfying intimate relationships should ideally provide happiness — and that if they do not, there must be something wrong with those relationships — seems to be greatly exaggerated. It also damages the precious relationships that we do have, by putting pressure on them as the make or break of our lives.

Love and friendship are important parts of our lives, but they are not the only source of happiness, and we change and develop as our lives continue. In fact this uncertainty is inherent in any relationship. Achieving the kind of internal validation which allows us to function and be happy on our own terms is what inventing your future is about.

Anthony Storr suggests that an inner world of fantasy must be regarded as part of an individual's biological inheritance. When an individual's subjective reality becomes completely divorced from the external reality, we call them mad. On the other hand, if we suppress the inner world too much we become totally compliant with external reality; we regard the external worlds as something to which we must adapt, so our individuality disappears and life becomes meaningless.

Pat had spent most of her life trying to please people. She seemed to be at her happiest when she was doing things for others. For a long period of time she worked in the same team. The group depended on her for solace, meditation and sacrifice. The work team was disbanded after six years and each team member assigned a personal project. The intention was to bring the team back together when they had finished. Pat found it hard to settle; she could not concentrate on her own. She began to offer help to others in finishing their projects, saying her own was the least important. The other team members, now working alone, found her behaviour irritating and began to avoid her. Her anxiety increased and made her even less comfortable. Without the approval of the group, she felt she had no purpose. Eventually her manager took her project away and gave her the job of co-ordinating all the projects. Pat could not invent her future. Her reality was other people's …

Being self-aware is not enough on its own. It is what we do and **how we apply the awareness** that enables or disables you from reality hacking.

courage, faith, bananas and yoghurt

It involves solving the right problem ... people starve not because there is not enough food in the world, but because it is not distributed. If we accept that we are all connected, we must then accept our impact on others and theirs on us. We have in the past constructed our realities to control our environment. In a more turbulent, ambiguous, future, we all need to free ourselves from the notion that we all know exactly what we are doing and how to do it. This would allow us to make errors without blame, without defences. Lowering our defences enables us to operate in a less selfish, more compassionate way, that addresses and encourages productive connectivity.

In order to grow, we need to learn rather than control;
not to demand solutions, but to ask questions;
to understand the situation and experience the moment.

This is understanding reality

WE CAN'T HACK IT UNTIL
WE UNDERSTAND IT ...

Feeling that as we grow and learn we can affect our futures increases our confidence and sense of well being ...

'Our deepest fear is not that we are
inadequate.
Our deepest fear is that we are
powerful beyond measure.
It is our light, not our darkness, that
most frightens us.
We ask ourselves, who am I to be
brilliant, gorgeous, talented and
fabulous?
Actually, who are you not to be?
You are a child of God. Your playing
small doesn't serve the world.
There is nothing enlightened about
shrinking so that other people
won't feel insecure around you.
We are born to manifest the glory of
God that is within us.
It's not just in some of us; it's in
everyone.
And as we let our own light shine,
we unconsciously give other people
permission to do the same.
As we are liberated from our own
fear, our presence automatically
liberates others.'

Marianne Williamson, as quoted by
Nelson Mandela, inauguration
address 1994

133

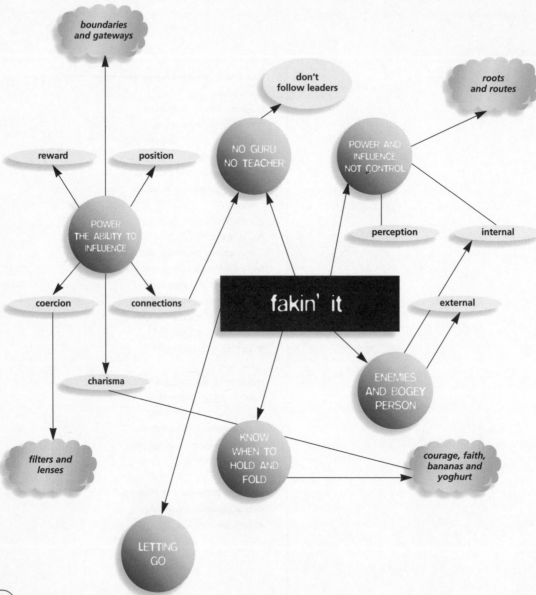

fakin' it

Presenting our future to others is our way of presenting ourselves to others. Our intent is usually to convince others of our purpose, but also to get approval. It is partly this need for approval that leads to us *fakin' it*. When we are not comfortable with our purpose, or the people we are communicating to, we often dissemble, or hide our feelings.

Fakin' it may sound like a negative judgement, but it is intended to describe the times we have to 'dissemble' knowingly or unknowingly to influence a situation or person, and keep ourselves 'safe'. It is about a stage in the reality hacking process when we are probably still in the confusion room, and are unsure of what is happening, or even what we want.

'It is only shallow people who do not judge by appearances'
Oscar Wilde

'Somewhere to run, nowhere to hide ...'
Eric Best

 LETTING GO ...

The biggest problem facing any aspiring reality hacker is fear of losing control. This is when we hit the big one.

OK, hear this:

control means letting go

you need to let go to hack reality

the only way to stay in control is to let go.

Imagine yourself as trying to stay in control by pulling very tightly on a rope, so that it is as taut as can be. Whilst that rope is taut, all your energies are focused on keeping it so, so they cannot be put to any other, more creative use. If you pull too tightly on the rope, it may snap anyway. Also, anyone can come along and cut it while you are so busy holding on.

On the other hand, if you decide when to slacken the rope and when to tighten it, and let go when you choose or think appropriate, you are in control of that rope.

THE ONLY WAY TO STAY IN CONTROL IS TO LET GO

Fakin' it is about the different ways we maintain the illusion of control, why our insecurities keep us doing it, and how we can use the understanding to invent futures, rather than maintain our personal status quo.

NO GURU, NO TEACHER ...

So if not within, where else do we perceive the answers?

Management and psychotherapy have been widely scorned by both the academic and business worlds for, respectively, their lack of scientific rigour and irrelevance to the real world of managing. Yet every year, more than seventy-five thousand students in the United States receive a Masters in Business Administration; American business spends $15 billion a year on outside advice from management consultants. Business has a seeming desire to simultaneously embrace and dismiss management gurus. This attitude can be partially traced to the gurus themselves. One the one hand, the relentlessly curious mind of Peter Drucker, whatever his advice, seems intent on making his readers think. Tom Peters on the other hand seems to want to belittle his audience, taking them from striving for excellence to five years later announcing that there were no excellent companies, and that he was talking rubbish in the past and they were stupid to believe him.

Michael Hammer has admitted that most attempts at re-engineering fail.

Like most people, experts have a deep need to create a human setting that needs them. Unlike many people, they have special opportunities to do so ...

John Kay in a recent newspaper article charted the growth of 'core competencies', one in the current range of panaceas on offer. He traced its lineage from a *Harvard Business Review* article by Gary Hamel and C.K. Prahalad, which was a popularisation of the resource-based theory of strategy. This can be defined in English as using and valuing what you have got. (Not a bad strategy for someone considering inventing their future ...) Resource-based theory in turn seems to have originated from a 1984 article by Bo Wernerfelt, and in turn the ideas it describes were first articulated in *The Theory of the Growth of the Firm* by Edith Penrose. This serves to highlight one of the problems with 'new ideas' — they are very rarely 'new', and may just be the same old same old repackaged, sometimes due to an academic or consultant's need to be delivering new 'product'. Cynical but true ...

Despite the vast outpouring of literature and the hero worship of business leaders like Jack Welch and Percy Barnevik, certainties in management theory and practice are few and far between. Few managers find themselves able to do without the psychological crutch of a consultant, an airport best-seller, or an article in *Harvard Business Review*. One manager said to me when asked why he was paying a well known 'guru' forty-five thousand pounds a day as a consultant, that he felt that he appeared to *be* somebody in the eyes of his colleagues because he was important enough to warrant the expenditure and exposure ... (I suspect exposure is probably a very accurate description).

This book has not set out to offer a true way or an answer.

The reality hacker's guru is the reality hacker him or herself

Of course there is no one right way to do anything — logic and reason tells us there cannot be just as no two managers, individuals or organisations are the same.

Self-help books have mushroomed in the last few years. Most of them purport to provide the panacea or answer to all your problems. (In fact, just what was your reason for buying this book?) Given the high stakes it is not surprising that managers buy bright ideas in the same way that people buy lottery tickets ... this might just be the one that hits the jackpot. Like lottery tickets few ideas do hit the jackpot. Organisations are not run by ideas, they are run by people, and what is a stunning proposal for one group of people may be totally inappropriate for another.

As Van Morrison suggests: 'no guru, no method, no teacher, just you and I in the garden ...'

So does it matter if we follow a fashion, or if a fashion fails?

It matters in a much deeper way than the loss of money expended. It matters more in the cynicism, demotivation and lack of belief which is present in large organisations who bear the scars of what Eileen Shapiro calls 'fad surfing'. One recent survey found that in the middle of massive restructuring half the employees in US companies were unable to articulate their company's strategy. If the members of the organisation don't have a clue about where they are heading or why, how can they be expected to give their all, do more with less and all the other company exhortations? Simple enough principle, but very rarely seen in the flesh.

In the same way that you cannot create a new company by demanding that the people in it behave differently, so you cannot expect that people can change the way they are simply by going on a leadership or time management course.

This has nothing to do with mission statements that are written on laminated plastic and used only to scrape the ice off the windscreen. This is about whether people know and believe in what they are part of.

The same is true of personal issues. Unless you understand why you became an accountant in the first place it is hard to know whether it is your job that makes you happy or sad. Or why a relationship feels less than positive: is it you or the person you are with?

What is it with management fads and fashions?

Why are supposedly rational managers so apparently addicted to the quick fix?

How is it that ideas which were original, clever and useful degenerate into snake oil?

Perhaps as life at work and at home becomes more complex, the pressures from both sides of our lives build up and demand another way, and it's just that we don't know it.

This of course obviates the need to look at how we currently operate and check out whether there is something fundamental in our approach that needs examining before we look for outside help.

We often speak or talk about being a 'good' parent. There is no such thing as a 'good' parent; only a good enough parent, who has done everything in their power for their child. Surely the same rules apply to managers of people and individuals on the rocky pathway of life? ... Our need to find unconditional love prompts us to look for the right answer that will please the organisation/manager/parent. What we really want is someone who will be different; who will accept us more openly and reward us for just being ourselves.

courage, faith, bananas and yoghurt

So we look outside of ourselves, sure that someone out there has the solution, and then if it doesn't work we can blame them not us. It's hard to have **the confidence to believe in our own solutions** when all around we are being sold 'the answer'.

So why do we look for answers everywhere except for inside ourselves?

Why do we look to people to give us answers and then dismiss them as arrogant, superficial and without understanding?

the changing rooms

We seek totality in an answer (witchcraft, fundamentalism) and, depending on the degree of our desperateness, we will accept almost anything ... The terror of the unknown makes us lose our curiosity, so we either look to others to be curious for us or we take a (seemingly) **no-risk** 'fast food' option.

ENEMIES AND BOGEYPERSONS ...

People vary considerably in the degree to which they can be their true selves in company. Some enviable mortals seem able to express whatever they are feeling in the presence of comparative strangers without fear of being rebuffed, disapproved of, contradicted or made to feel foolish. Others find it hard to be truly themselves (sometimes they do not even know what that is), even in the presence of their friends, partners or family. Sometimes these individuals have a need to be alone and create a 'safe' world for themselves. Where this comes from could be explained or postulated in many ways, but whatever the reasons, it has insecurity at its heart.

roots and routes

Sometimes the method of *fakin' it* is some form of projection ... our emotions are too difficult or dangerous for us to harbour within us, so we project them on to someone else. Sometimes people who have trouble admitting to their own difficulties or fears take up their time rescuing others so that they won't have to deal with themselves. Some people deliberately take up jobs or roles where they won't have to disclose as much as others disclose to them. That puts them out of risk of exposure.

So who do you THINK you are exposed to?

What do you THINK 'they' can do to you?

What CAN 'they' do to you?

Often at crisis moments in our lives we find ourselves on the edge of a precipice, with no choice but to accept the reality of our situation. It is at such moments that we can really get a hold of which of our fears are real and which are perceived; which we really should be scared of, and which we can ignore.

Unfortunately, instead of seeing the crisis as a moment of discovery, we are too busy panicking about what might be, rather than what is. We also keep people in our heads as bogeypersons long after they have ceased to have any relation to us.

What creates a bogeyperson?

'I've been freed from the self
that pretends to be someone,
And in becoming no-one,
I begin to live.
It is worth while dying,
to find out what life is'
T.S. Eliot

Most of the time we don't know. All we are aware of is that someone feels like a threat to us. Just as children are scared of the dark, so we carry our internal enemies with us, truly or falsely. Sometimes we need people to be 'bad', so that we can write them off. To do this we punish and blame. Sometimes we make ourselves the bogeyperson, and see ourselves as victims of our own wrongdoing.

A great deal of the insecurity that comes with fakin' stems from a sense of loss of control. In order to create control, we create the illusion of control by fakin' it. Bogeypersons, internal and external, are one method of doing this.

# POWER AND INFLUENCE, NOT CONTROL ...

So what forms does this dissembling take?

Well, let's get back to that word *control*. All perceived wisdom, science, social and economic structures stem from the need to control, and to be seen to be in control.

These conventional norms are counterproductive in the turbulent world of reality hacking. We lack concepts for coping with incoherence and ambiguity. Those people whose confidence and competence is defined by the ability to control, may find themselves with anxiety a constant companion, and burn out a frequent destiny.

Acknowledging uncertainty means
acknowledging that one is unsure about
what causes different effects, and this leaves us feeling unable to
'control' the situation, or 'solve' the problem.

By refusing to accept the uncertainty of a situation and what can be done about it, both individuals and organisations are inviting loss of faith: confusion and ineffectiveness come about as a result of 'knee-jerk' reactions to a fear of losing control.

the changing rooms

We feel out of control and immediately respond by pulling the rope tight, and shutting our eyes to what is really going on. Most of the time our response is completely incomprehensible to the people around us, particularly if it has resulted in a clamp down on others. For example, I recently shouted at my daughter about the state of her room. 'Times don't change,' she said to me, in a very calm voice. 'Before I respond to you, I need to know whether you are really angry with me over this; whether you are pre-menstrual; or whether you are stressed about something else and are coming down hard on me because you don't know how to solve your other problem.'

Yes, this is a true story, and, after my shock response, followed by a short two second, 'how dare she', I burst out laughing.

She was right of course; my frustration with another issue had resulted in a feeling of loss of control, and I was subconsciously trying to regain control by pushing her.

Our cultural view of an 'effective' individual has been the one who came up with an 'answer'. Assigning sole responsibility to an individual for what happens in his or her life also helps perpetuate the belief that control is attainable. According to this norm, an unfulfilling life is down to the individual's failure to control life's situations, rather than the fallibility of the concept of controllability. All of the recent self-help movement seems to point to 'taking control of your life', and assert that we are responsible for everything we are or are not.

While this does discourage us from blaming others for our circumstances, it also leaves the individual very much on his or her own ... 'that's your problem ... '

To invent our futures we need to be able to discover balance between
a desperate desire for locked down control and the
need to take appropriate responsibility for self and others.

We are not totally responsible for control, but
we are responsible for our reactions to it.

There is a difference between control
and personal power.

Reality hacking is about appropriate use of
personal power resources, not control.

Power as a concept leaves us
very ambivalent.
We confuse power with control.

We want power and we continually seek it out, but we don't like to admit it. We also feel very uncomfortable about *not* having it ... that is exactly what I mean by fakin' it ...

We are not very honest with ourselves most of the time, and end up disguising or hiding what we want and feel. The long-term effect of this is that we cannot invent our future, because we cannot truly own up to what we want, without feeling bad or guilty or many of those emotions which block us.

POWER – THE ABILITY TO INFLUENCE ...

So,
if not from without,
what is the source of
our strength and power?

In order to hack reality, we need to know what resources we have at our disposal: not how much authority we have, but what we can use in order to make a difference to a situation.

> **POWER FOR THE REALITY HACKER IS THE ABILITY TO INFLUENCE ...**
> **... NO MORE NO LESS**

Every interaction we have with people involves manipulating the way we speak or behave, consciously or subconsciously, in order to influence an outcome.

Manipulation as a word or concept gets a very bad press. It is the intent behind the behaviour that renders it positive or negative either for ourselves or for the individual(s) on the receiving end. Manipulation is about how we adjust the way we speak and act to get what we want. We start very young, and are very aware of how children manipulate us to get their way. Most of their behaviour is intuitive and they are unaware at a conscious level of doing it. The same is true of many of our 'grown-up' interactions.

We instinctively know which buttons to press in others to get what we want, as they do in us. When this button pressing leaves us feeling abused or betrayed in some way, we use the word manipulated negatively.

If we break down the things we use to influence with, they fall into six main categories, or power resources:

expert power

reward power

coercive power

referent power

legitimate power

charismatic power

My power resource will be the reason why I am able to influence you. It's important not to confuse power with authority. Authority does not reside with the individual; it belongs to the organisation or institution which bestows it. Many people when they talk of feeling disempowered mean they feel they have no authority. But authority is not confined to people in organisations. It is what we feel as parents, partners and customers. As such, it is limiting to increase your level of influence by trying to increase levels of authority — what the organisation giveth, it taketh away.

Power resources, or bases, live with the individual,
          and as such are the only thing that is important
     in terms of hacking our realities.

A power base is a reason for others to allow
their behaviour to be influenced.

A power base, therefore, exists in the mind of the person who obeys, not in the mind of the person who commands; *my* power base is *your* reason for compliance. We can increase our personal power by increasing the number or the visible importance of our power bases.

So what are these power bases?

One which we all have is expert power, power based on knowledge or experience.

Some individuals become recognised for their unique personal knowledge or wisdom.

KNOWLEDGE IS *NOT* POWER: the power lies in your ability to *use*, *apply* or *interpret* the knowledge.

This is such a key precept that I am tempted to write it twice. We have inordinate respect and deference for those with knowledge, such as doctors, and thereby hand them power and, therefore, influence.

sowing and growing

The actual information is not the influence. In the same way, access to the Internet and all its information is not in itself power. The power lies in knowing what you want from the information, and being able to apply it. So this deification of the Net will collapse if people cannot understand or apply the technology.

Expert power can be easily won and lost. What sort of things lose it, and what sort of things enhance it?

LOSE EXPERT POWER	ENHANCE EXPERT POWER
be wrong	admit when you don't know something (but not too often)
	be right
not keep up to date	stay learning
play games	be straight
withhold knowledge	share it
threaten	be non-judgemental and patient
give too much data	give only what is relevant – what people need
	check understanding
talk in jargon	be accessible — talk in a language people can relate to
inappropriate waffle	big systemic picture

Expert power is only power when people can access your knowledge or experience base, otherwise it is static knowledge that resides in your head.

**Closely related to the expert power base in terms of
the way your knowledge is communicated, is the**

reward power base.

This is power based on incentive — I would be able to influence you if you perceived personal benefit.

Many times we think we are giving people reasons why they should do something, when we are not thinking what an incentive would be for them. Key to having an effective reward power base is understanding what a reward would look like to the person we are trying to influence.

We are very good at projecting our own needs for reward on others, rather than thinking what motivates another. This is understanding another person's reality, and then using that understanding to persuade and influence. Psychological reward is the delivery or the promise of the delivery of a psychological benefit, such as security, recognition, or challenge. The desire for recognition is one of the main motives of high achievers; conversely, lack of recognition is the most frequent cause of dissatisfaction amongst managers in large organisations.

It appears that many managers, even though they crave it, are wary of giving too much praise, and err in the opposite direction. Or it may be that managers identify reward power with the formal system (which they cannot influence) and ignore psychological rewards (which they can influence).

Lack of incentive, or perceived incentive, or even the wrong incentive, often starts us on a reality hacking trail. It isn't just at the workplace we need the reward, it's in every part of our lives.

If our relationships do not fulfil the promise we expect
        – that is, give us a 'reward' —
                          we feel trapped and power-less.

We need to know,
        as part of inventing a future for ourselves,
                what constitutes a reward for ourselves.

What is it about work,
relationships, interests, that
makes us feel we are getting
something back?

It is important to talk in terms of *benefits* rather than features. If we go to buy a washing machine, we are not interested in how many buttons it has — we want to know what it will do for us. It is this understanding of what is in it for the person you are trying to influence that allows you to influence. Good salespeople ask questions about people's life-styles and their habits before selling their product: then they sell in the framework of the individual, having established what is important to them. They describe the product in the language and culture of the person they are trying to influence. For example, there is no point in selling someone a washing machine that saves time if speed is not an issue for him or her.

The effect that showing an understanding of people has on your ability to influence cannot be overestimated. An effective reality hacker knows how to package what they want to say in the framework of the listener: they know how to hit the target.

Understanding other people's frameworks is about hacking *their* realities, in order to achieve *yours*. We need to know what benefits we want from a particular scenario, not just what the features are.

Hacking other people's realities demands getting into their heads without getting out of yours. This in turn means you have to be very aware of *your* reality ... It's a challenge.

The most commonly used power base is coercive power, power based on fear.

This means that you will do what I want you to do because I have frightened you with vague and nasty threats if you don't do what I ask.

This comes in many formats. At one time, a well-known sales organisation would only hire people over six feet tall to intimidate their customers. Some people intimidate by shouting, swearing, banging doors, or more subtly by withdrawal of favours.

Psychological coercion — the withdrawal or the threat of the withdrawal of a psychological benefit — is common in organisations and social groups. Being sent to Coventry (withdrawal of social membership), the threat of redundancy (withdrawal of security), or lack of promotion (ego and growth benefits) or close supervision (autonomy concern). All these are common examples of psychological coercion.

We often underestimate the extent to
        which we use psychological coercion.

One of the hardest lessons to learn about ourselves is that others are
        frightened of us.

This is a very dangerous power base, and the most you can hope to get from using it is resentful compliance. You usually only get exactly what you asked for. If people are exposed to fear for long periods of time, they either become inured and ignore it, deliver the minimum requirement or mutiny. Being on the receiving end of someone else's coercive power usually makes it very difficult for us to create our own reality.

Is the fear real?

Is it self-generated?

Can we overcome it?

Use of coercive power usually results in dysfunction,

either ours or the person we are trying to affect.

Understanding this is key to

developing and realising our future ...

Referent power rests on who you know, not what you know.

People will often comply with another's wishes simply because they like the person. In addition, if you know powerful people, you can borrow their power. In a work situation, typically, the power borrowed is positional power:

'We must have the report typed up by Thursday, as the MD needs it for Friday's Board meeting.'

Power can also be borrowed from institutions, people or objects outside the organisation.

Conversely, if you are in a position in which others will want to borrow your power, this provides you with a power base over them. People who hold senior positions, or provide role models which others seek to emulate, thereby exercise referent power over those who seek to imitate them. The MD can establish that formal suits are expected in head office simply by wearing a formal suit on all occasions.

USING SOMEONE ELSE'S POWER DOES NOT INCREASE YOUR OWN

If anything, using another's power decreases yours, and enhances someone else's. If you use someone else's power to create your future, you need to consider how much impact *their* dynamic has on *your* reality.

One way to develop your own referent power is to develop networks of people to whom you can go to obtain advice, stimulation, ideas, etc.

This form of referent power is key for flexible, connected reality hackers, who need many connections to enable them to see the 'big picture'.

Legitimate power, too, derives from both structural and individual factors.

When power derives from the organisation structure, it is known as 'authority', or position power. Personal legitimate power is somewhat less common. In a democracy, individuals are theoretically equal, and thus custom is less likely to identify particular individuals as worthy of obedience. However, there are some people to whom others knowingly and willingly concede the right to be influential because of their standing in society. Examples might includes those with famous friends or family, great wealth, or outstanding performance in areas of central importance either to the organisation or to society at large.

Olympic medal winners appear on TV chat shows, an opportunity to exercise power denied to most of us; members of the royal family, lacking any formal position in the organisations they visit, may nevertheless influence events if only by showing interest in a particular issue.

This power base is harder to increase than the others, but is probably of less use to a reality hacker because it is based on position, and in the future worlds this may be so changeable that what was perceived as a position of power one day may be gone the next.

It is also depends on others' perception of 'power', rather than whether that is truly the case; that is they have the power to influence, rather than just the trappings. For example, governments are perceived to have the power to influence, and many people become politicians because they want to affect society. In reality, the bureaucratic systems may get in the way of the individual achieving change.

The final form of personal power is charismatic power — the capacity to influence others through the sheer impact of your personality.

In developing the confidence to develop and implement our own futures, this is usually at the centre, either because we need it to make the leap of faith, or because it happens as result of increased confidence …

courage, faith, bananas and yoghurt

Charismatic power is the ability to get people to do what you want, by the impact of you. Many people think they are charismatic, very few are truly charismatic. However, we all have the principles of charisma inside of us. To invent our future, and make it happen, we need to be able to get in touch with that part of us, and use it.

When we think of charismatic people, we usually think of politicians or people in the public eye. For example, Martin Luther King, John F. Kennedy, Nelson Mandela. All these people share things in common in terms of the way they behave. It is these traits that the reality hacker needs to focus on and use:

a clear vision of what they want to achieve

conviction in their beliefs

passion when describing what they want

the ability to understand what other people need, and address them appropriately

the ability to inspire

enthusiasm and excitement (very infectious)

There is nothing more attractive than a person who believes passionately in what they are saying. We are drawn to people who 'believe'. They seem safe, strong and secure; and maybe some of their belief will rub off on us ... Confidence begets confidence; we have to take that leap of faith sometime, believe in ourselves in order to begin the increasing spiral ...

Charisma, as with any other power base, is not in itself enough: it must also be seen to meet some need in the people.

The most potent cocktail of power bases is the combination of expert power, reward power and charismatic power — someone who

knows what people want

gives only relevant and useful
knowledge in a language that does not
threaten or confuse

presents the information in a way that
reflects and connects to the
framework of the listener, and is
perceived by the listener to be of
benefit to them

presents with conviction, enthusiasm
and belief

Well, we don't get lots of opportunities to combine them, but we get more than we use …

One word of warning ... power bases exist in the minds of the influenced. In order to enhance your power bases, you **must** communicate them. The most common method is to assume that you have the power. However, the more obvious you make the power, the less likely it is to be willingly obeyed. If you march into your office, shouting 'You will do what I say because I am the **manager**', the corporate cartoonists will have a field-day and you will lose power.

If, on the other hand, you just assume that your reasonable requests will be heeded, then you will probably get what you want and, in the process, enhance your power. The way you use your power bases will, therefore, increase (or erode) your power.

Power can be used in three general senses:

to achieve action

> **to prevent action**

>> **to shape attitudes.**

The more visible and the more coercive the use of power, the more likely it is to be resisted. Pressure typically creates counter-pressure.

For that reason power works best when it is used invisibly. If you do not notice that you are being influenced you certainly will not resist. The most subtle use is, therefore, in shaping attitudes. If you can influence others' attitudes such that they only want what you want, then you have no need to coerce.

In organisations, the use of power political activity — may be either overt or covert. Overt political activity is usually associated with the goals of the organisation, whilst covert activity is often linked to personal goals.

Behind the use of power there are always moral questions:

Am I right to use power in this way?

Is this management, or manipulation?

Authors vary widely in their definitions of the moral limits to power. Some regard only position power as legitimate; others see overt action in pursuit of organisational goals as legitimate, whatever the power base; still others regard as legitimate any use of power which has the overt consent of the people who comply. It is important for any individual to think through his or her own definition of the limits to their use of power. Power can certainly corrupt without a clear moral code to limit and define its appropriate uses.

THE CORRUPTION BEGINS NOT IN POWER, BUT IN IGNORANCE ABOUT THAT POWER

The reality hacker has to look at power resources then develop them and use them. To create and implement our future, we need to understand what we have, and what other people need. It is one step to decide what we want from our future, but it is by being able to positively influence others and situations that we build and develop our confidence for the future ...

KNOW WHEN TO HOLD AND FOLD ...

Hacking reality demands the ability to see beyond the fantasy of worlds we have created, whether they are there to protect us or help us cope. We all need fantasy, but it is not possible to invent your own future if you are grounded in fantasy alone, as any future will be based on that perception. We have to get beyond whatever it is we are doing to fake it, to the reality of us.

This is not about change through insight or making a new relationship, or acquiring knowledge. It isn't even about finding contentment through solving a particular problem. It is about an inner change of attitude.

Part of the control myth that we believe in suggests that when we accept things they overpower us in some way. However, it is only by accepting them that we can take up an attitude towards them. By keeping quiet, repressing nothing, remaining attentive, and accepting reality, we become able to hack it. Forcing everything to go the way we think it ought to go gives us *less* not more power or control.

THE ONLY WAY TO STAY IN CONTROL IS TO LET GO

The idea of control seriously limits our ability to hack reality. The fantasy runs deep, but it is a fantasy.

When we actually let go of the reins of a dilemma, we frequently see it for what it really is, and the moment of insight about what to do, comes not from action but from standing still. This may also mean that we set out hopefully on a journey towards a destination at which one never arrives ... It is the journey that is the reality.

'If you sum up what people tell you about their experiences, you can formulate it this way: They came to themselves, they could accept themselves, they were able to become reconciled to themselves, and thus were reconciled to adverse circumstances and events'
Carl Jung

167

Reality hacking demands an ability to utilise our personal power resources to act and make decisions. It is also part of the confidence building required to make the leap that changes the way we are operating, and follow new futures. We can only do this if we have the confidence that we *can* do it. The confidence begins when we realise that we *do* have the ability to influence our circumstances through the resources we have as individuals, not the authority from external sources.

'We are lived by powers we
pretend to understand'
W.H. Auden

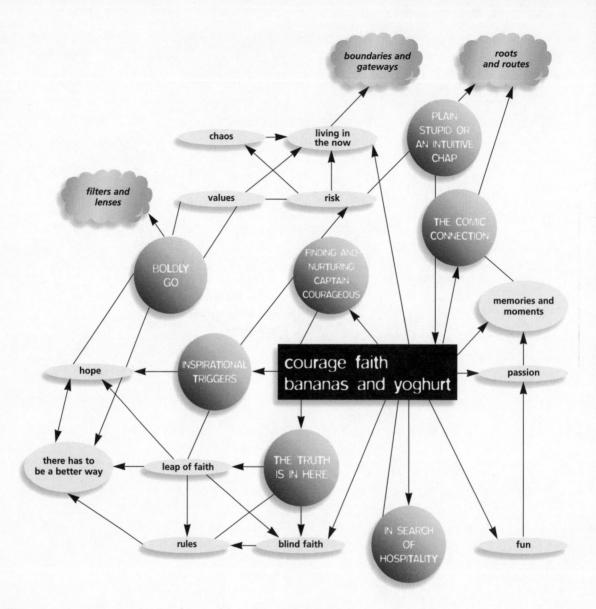

boundaries and
gateways

roots
and routes

chaos → living in
the now

PLAIN
STUPID OR
AN INTUITIVE
CHAP

filters and
lenses

values — risk

THE COMIC
CONNECTION

BOLDLY
GO

FINDING AND
NURTURING
CAPTAIN
COURAGEOUS

memories and
moments

INSPIRATIONAL
TRIGGERS

hope

courage faith
bananas and yoghurt

passion

there has to
be a better way

leap of faith

THE TRUTH
IS IN HERE

IN SEARCH
OF
HOSPITALITY

rules → blind faith

fun

courage, faith, bananas and yoghurt

GREAT FAITH … GREAT DOUBT
… GREAT EFFORT

... three qualities necessary for Zen training

So what happens to us when we know
we need to move on,
and find that first step so difficult?

Or when we feel so caught up in a
situation that we can't think straight?

What is it that makes us take that step
into the dark, into the unknown?

Is there any way we can increase
our ability to leap?

'Through purely logical thinking
we can attain no knowledge
whatsoever of the empirical
world'
Albert Einstein

This section of the book, by its very nature, will ask you more questions than it will provide answers. Courage and faith are so difficult to grab hold of that we need to ask ourselves many questions to develop our thoughts. They are not part of any training course or academic syllabus. Yet if we don't understand them we cannot take up the future we want.

We may not even be able to imagine or invent it, we have so little faith in ourselves.

Courage and faith is not about skill development. It is about getting in touch with a wholly spiritual part of ourselves that we usually ignore or take for granted. Don't head for another section yet, this isn't about religion, it is about inner soul: the things that we can't usually describe, the profound feelings we have but barely understand.

They are what will allow us to invent and enjoy our realities, or prevent us from so doing.

All sections in this book are interdependent and connected. In a way, this section holds a special place in the reality hacker's heart, because it is the deep commitment part of us that we know so little about, and can rationalise so little.

'Give me a fruitful error any time, full of seeds, bursting with its own corrections. You can keep your sterile truths for yourself'
Vilfredo Pareto

COMMITMENT IS THE SOUL OF THE ASPIRING HACKER

Because of its nature, the thoughts and comments are likely to be less sequential, more random, and there are likely to be more questions. It reflects this part of our lives: questioning and trusting; fuzzy and courageous; intuitive and passionate.

FINDING AND NURTURING CAPTAIN COURAGEOUS …

Reality hacking is about working out the difference between fantasy and reality, and how courage and faith exist in both.

Believing in yourself is the X file of management and life …
if you don't have the faith, the courage is hard to find
(let alone the bananas and yoghurt …).

'The winds of grace blow all the time. All we need to do is set our sails'
Ramakrishna

sowing and growing

The problem lies is not being able to see an answer or at least a palatable one as soon as we might like. More often than not there is not a conventional answer or even one at all … sometimes the answer is an acceptance of reality; so reality hacking becomes reality realising …

'However, some wind smells better than others …'
Dee Hahn Rollins

Many of the issues that we struggle with don't have great plans as solutions. They demand that we see things as they are. The creativity required to invent a future comes after we have had this realisation, and can then be creative and excited about how we hack that reality.

It sounds almost as if we have achieved nothing, and at first glance doesn't look as exciting as solving a problem. Sometimes the hardest thing to do is accept yourself; it takes more courage to do that than invent a fantasy …

How do we become courageous?

the changing rooms

Courage is about believing in yourself enough to do whatever you feel is necessary to achieve what you think is right. But the step required to commit ourselves, and by its very nature take a leap into the unknown, should not be underestimated. We can only have faith in ourselves if we have thought something through and wrestled with both it and ourselves in the confusion room.

OK, let's assume that we have grappled with and are about to make a decision that requires a leap of faith. It may be a yes to us, but it may be a no to someone else.

Are you prepared to pay the cost?

Does that cost keep us from making the leap?

Sometimes we need encouragement that that decision will not cut us off from the people we respect and love.

We have to get to a point where we believe that the promise will outlive the cost that the promise is so great; that we can run the risk. Often we don't know …

'There is a cost and a promise to every choice we make'
Verna Dozier

How do we know that we are doing the right thing?

Some people have graphic visions. Some just know what they want to do at that moment. Sometimes it just 'fits' with something as yet unnamed, with what intuitively feels right. Sometimes when we cannot put a name to or box a thought we are prevented from being able to label and therefore describe and justify our actions.

At times like this we look for Captain Courageous in others, whether they are partners, friends or therapists. We are not necessarily asking them to make the commitment for us, more to reassure us that everything will be okay after we have made that commitment. They can say it, but nothing they say will actually reassure us deep down, because we know that we will have to experience it for ourselves.

We need to touch the Captain in ourselves, and give ourselves permission to get it wrong ... that is the really courageous part.

If we follow someone else's belief, it does not build our inner confidence because it cannot. The original thought did not come from us. The decision to commit to someone else's faith, for example, could be argued as a personal decision you have taken. Whether it gives you inner faith and courage will depend on the motivation behind the decision.

What are the dynamics between you and the person you want to follow? If your relationship with someone is dependent, then the decision you make to follow them increases your dependency, rather than your courage, quotient.

Do you know what it is that stops you feeling that you can do it yourself?

Have you ever asked yourself the question?

What is it that the person you are seeking leadership from can give you that you can't give yourself?

What would be the worst thing that could happen if you followed your instinct without anyone else's reassurance?

THE TRUTH IS IN HERE …

We manage to get through life without making any really major mistakes like putting a fork in our eye or walking out of a window instead of a door, so why do we not trust ourselves more?

SOMETIMES YOU HAVE TO BE SEEN TO BE BELIEVED; OTHER TIMES YOU HAVE TO BELIEVE TO BE SEEN.

(This is a complex sentence … I am not sure I understand it myself, but I like the sound of it.)

Some people can just jump into a situation, some people have to be able to imagine themselves there, or visualise it in some way. Some of us have to have concrete proof or validation before we can move. Sometimes our need for concreteness can diminish as we grow in confidence; or we begin to realise that we need less concrete data to move.

There are also times when we have to accept that nothing, however great, will make us feel good or confident. If we can allow ourselves to stay down there, and roll in the mud for a while, knowingly, we stand a better chance of coming out the other end. Actually giving ourselves permission to stay there is about believing in yourself enough to give yourself space.

*roots
and routes*

What are the chances of you believing in others if you don't believe in yourself?

Well, plenty actually, and therein lies the problem. When it becomes easier to believe in others than yourself, the warning bells should ring.

When this happens it becomes very difficult to take things on and commit to them, and suddenly responsibility becomes a problem. Suddenly it's a lot easier to do what someone else wants than take a chance yourself. Let someone else do it. But then it becomes their reality, not yours.

'If you want a guarantee, buy a toaster'
Clint Eastwood character in
The Rookie

You can't invent your own future, if someone else has decided it for you.

This is the decision crunch point:

Now you get to decide whether you really want to hack your reality or not.

Even if you actively choose to hand over all responsibility for your faith and courage to another, that is deciding and committing to a reality. It's a limited one, but you made the decision and, if you commit to it, that is your future. It's the active commitment that matters. You must own responsibility for your actions. That's where the courage comes in.

When it is put like that, we cannot conceive of consciously handing over our life to someone else, and yet we do it on a regular basis dishonestly and subconsciously …

So why is it so hard for us to believe that we can make the big decisions for ourselves; that we can have the faith?

It's like being afraid of the dark. We all fear it, but find it hard to justify the feeling.

Taking a leap of faith will always imply leaping into the dark …
… it must do by its very nature, but therein also lies the promise.

There is also the risk of losing something we enjoy if we talk about it or admit to it. We seem to have an irrational, or maybe quite rational for some of us, fear that if anyone else knows that we are happy or enjoying something, they might take it away. There almost seems to be a culture of self-denigration. On the television, for example, presenters say 'look at me, I'm the emperor and I've got no clothes on … see how vulnerable I am' … We actually say we are doing something stupid before anyone else can, even if it isn't really stupid. At school people swear blind that they haven't done a stroke of work when you know really that they have; but saying you have means that some success might be expected of you as a result of doing the work, and that would be a very hard thing to live up to. The overall message we are left with is 'don't change … (or if you do don't tell anybody)'.

'We are what we pretend to be, so we must be careful about what we pretend to be'
Kurt Vonnegut

It's hard to invent or believe in your own future when these dynamics are all around you.

How do we control our minds?

Sometimes we are able to choose what we want to do, and then find a way to make ourselves do it. But we also spend our lives in search of schemes that will give us self-control. There is an important part of our 'self' that has as its purpose keeping us from changing too rapidly.

If we changed our minds too often, or too recklessly, we could never know what we wanted next. We might never get much done, because we would not be able to depend on ourselves.

We do need courage and faith to break free sometimes, but we also need to know when to have the courage to stay where we are. Doing that knowingly is very different from just letting things happen. Hacking reality means knowing the difference between the two and acting accordingly. We need to pay attention not just to the things that we want, but to what we want ourselves to be.

'"Supposing a tree fell down Pooh, when we were underneath it?"
"Supposing it didn't," said Pooh after careful thought Piglet was comforted by this'
A.A. Milne

Sometimes we need to know we are
wanted
elsewhere
to enable us to stay
where we are.

It is very hard not to denigrate the torture of decision-making in its initial change flushes.

How do we deal with having made the decision, and then being disappointed with its initial outcome?

Back to the X files ... it's hard to believe in something that, best case, no one else seems to; or, worst case, everyone thinks you are crazy to believe in.

the changing rooms

The business streets are littered with tales of entrepreneurs at whom everyone sniggered (and in some cases continue to snigger at). How did/do they get past the need for certain success that stops you taking the risk?

Sometimes you have to just do it ...

and hope ...

and maybe get it wrong ...

break the rules.

Sometimes we need permission to let out some of the wilder thoughts that circulate in our minds.

Having the thoughts does not render us 'mad', but surely if we express those wilder thoughts people will think we are mad? Quite often our imagination has done the work for us, but we don't believe it.

For example, if I suggested that when you read you are being creative you would probably feel puzzled. How can a seemingly passive act can render you creative? If I asked you to imagine that you had just walked into a room and you saw a woman standing in it, I am sure that you would be able to describe both the room and the woman.

… I bet you did as you were reading this …

Well that sounds like your imagination being creative to me …

It happens spontaneously for us;

we just need to trust it and use it.

We are creative in this way all the time but have no sense of effort. When we think about how to release some of our creative energy in order to invent our future, we need to be aware that we create more than we actually know; so we need to find a way of getting in touch with that part of us. Too often too many of us think that only special people can 'have an idea' and that they need special conditions to do it. We worship genius. None of us can draw a straight line.

READING THE GAPS ...

'The notes I handle no better
than many pianists. The pauses
between the notes — ah that is
where the art resides!'
Artur Schnabel

When we look at a comic strip we are able to make a move from one picture to another and make the transition necessary to understand what is going on in the white space between the pictures.

Much of reality hacking has to do with reading the white space between thoughts, speech and actions. We make the intuitive leaps without realising we have done it.

Reality hacking is about being more aware of ourselves so that we can be more thoughtful about our forays into white space, and use the fact that if we are doing it all the time then maybe the leaps of faith are not as big as we imagine them to be.

There isn't always a conventional answer, and sometimes there isn't an answer at all ... sometimes you have to ignore what everyone else is saying, ignore the noise around you and just do it.

There is a story told about something J.R.R. Tolkien did while he was marking a student's work. He noticed a white sheet that had accidentally slipped in between two of the student's pages. He drew a line across the sheet and wrote:

'Once upon a time in a hole in the earth, lived a hobbit …'

He then continued to mark the paper.

What is important about this white space story is that some time later, Tolkien recognised the beginning of something creative, and came back to it. The rest is history. He had faith in his white space experience. We need to become more aware and trusting of our white space connections, and use them to go forward …

Sometimes white space is there when we sleep. Sometimes it helps to let a problem sink into our subconscious rather than force it into the open ... We wake in the morning and the solution or insight is there. As a Hungarian laxative advertisement said: 'While you sleep, it does the work.'

The mind works in mysterious ways ...

... if we only let it ...

'There is a crack in everything, that's

how the light gets in ...' — Leonard Cohen

open those cracks a little wider ...

PLAIN STUPID OR INTUITIVE LEAP ...

There are plenty of times when people make a giant leap or commit to something that seems unreal or stupid. Whether it is unachievable or not depends on the frame in which they set up the idea. For example, nine women cannot produce a baby in one month ... although you could probably find a logician who could tell you that he could make it happen!

'You can only find truth with logic if you have already found truth without it'
G.K. Chesterton

So how do we distinguish between plain stupid and a creative intuitive leap?

I'm not sure we always can. I think our fear of plain stupid is so strong that we sometimes label thoughts plain stupid when they are just scary. Because we protect ourselves so well it is logically unlikely that we will think of something completely stupid ... outrageous maybe, but stupid is probably more of a fear than a reality.

Fear of looking stupid is so common and often overpowering that we need to acknowledge it rather than dismiss it. It's there, accept it, see it for what it is.

It is also at this stage that we need to consider what is behind our desire. We need to know the concept not the answer.

If we start off with the answer
we are limiting not only our options
but also our ability to think ...

... it will focus us down too early
and will definitely activate our
arrival at premature closure.

THE COMIC CONNECTION ...

Have you ever wondered how, when you are reading comic strips, you manage to get from one picture to the next with very little exposition? We take in a great deal more than we think when we look at pictures. The art of the effective comic strip writer is to communicate through space not substance. We make the intuitive leap across the white space to the next frame. We make a subconscious connection between frames, and understand their interrelationship.

Comics are a perfect metaphor for reality hacking in that they are a form of storytelling in which no philosophies, no ways of seeing and no movements are out of bounds. Their success depends on clear outline and limited detail to distract the eye.

The juxtaposition of frames is crucial. The reality of life is distilled into its simplest line form, yet we understand the form and the icons completely. When cartoonists abstract an idea into a cartoon they don't so much eliminate detail as focus on specific details, the details which matter.

By stripping down an idea to its simplest form, the artist can amplify meaning in a way that a detailed photograph can't. It isn't a way of drawing, it's a way of *seeing*.

The simplicity of the cartoon allows us to see the message, not the messenger.

'Bob was as perplexed as a hacker who means to access
T:flw.quid55328.com\aaakk/ch@ung
but gets
T:\flw.quidaaakk/ch@ung
by mistake'
Ken Krattenmaker

SEE ANY CONNECTIONS? ...

189

All of us perceive the world through the experience of our senses; yet our senses can only reveal a world that is fragmented and incomplete. Our perception of reality is an act of faith, based on fragments. As infants we find it hard to commit that act of faith, and if we can't see it, touch it, hear it, feel it, or smell it, then it isn't there. Some of us keep that belief for a long time: it is often what stops us being able to invent our future, as we can only perceive the present.

The game 'peek-a-boo' plays on this idea. Gradually children learn that even though the actual sight of mummy comes and goes, mummy is still there. The phenomenon of observing the parts but perceiving the whole is called closure. Every day, we mentally complete, or close, that which is incomplete, based on past experience. In recognising and relating to people, we depend on our learnt ability of closure.

In an incomplete world, we depend on closure.

Sometimes we accept closure too soon and block off any newness.

We recreate the same reality we had.

To capture the spark of reality hacking we need to go to the gutter.

The gutter is the space between pictures in comic strips
        where our imagination takes two separate images,
    connects them, and forms them into a single idea.

Nothing is seen between the panels, but experience tells you
            something must be there
                    (just like mummy playing peek-a-boo).

In movies, as well as comic strips, we understand more from a curtain blowing in the wind over an open window then the image suggests. To become reality hackers we need to get in touch with the part of us that makes these unconscious connections.

'He spoke with the wisdom that can only come from experience, like a guy who went blind because he looked at a solar eclipse without one of those boxes with a pinhole in it, and now goes around the country speaking at high schools about the dangers of looking at a solar eclipse without one of those boxes with a pinhole in it'
Joseph Romm

We need to be able to see

where the white space in our lives is ...

... jump in ...

... and make the intuitive connections ...

INSPIRATIONAL TRIGGERS …

A great deal of the courage needed to make the leaps comes from triggers which inspire an idea or train of thought.

Being inspired makes us excited and confident.

We always begin our journey in trepidation, fearful that we won't get inspired. Like most things we wish for, the wishing does not always make it happen, and, if we are seeking too hard, we miss the blindingly obvious …

How did you read the title
of this section —
courage, faith, bananas and yoghurt?

What were your thoughts on the title?

DID IT INTRIGUE YOU?

Did you think it was weird?

What does it mean?

DOES IT MATTER?

We often use phrases to capture moments or feelings. The title was something which meant something to me and inspired me to write the pieces that relate to this section. It means something to me but very little to anyone else.

It may have stirred your curiosity, or irritated you. Either way, it will help if you can ask yourself why you have a particular reaction.

Understanding this will help you to decide what forms your need, what things trigger your imagination, and how you can access them, or at least know the kind of things that are likely to trigger and inspire.

An individual who feels inspired is not making any decisions or comparing one thought with another. They are accepting their first thought (like Mozart putting his music straight down on paper as he felt it, believing in his creation). Inspiration does not come with rehearsal or planning; it comes because we allow it to.

The inspirations are everywhere, within and without. Only you can take them and use them.

'Whence and how they come, I know not; nor can I force them. Those that please me I retain in the memory, and I am accustomed, as I have been told, to hum them'
Mozart (writing about his ideas)

'The only Zen you experience at the tops of mountains is the Zen you bring'
– Robert M. Pirsig

We look for patterns sometimes where there are none;
and miss them sometimes when there are …

IN PURSUIT OF SPONTANEITY ...

Are we waiting
for the thrill to return?

We search for 'the thrill' in everyday life, even when we don't really know what a thrill might look like for us. Sometimes when you are that busy looking you don't see anything.

Perfect happiness, that feeling of harmony between inner and outer worlds, is only transient. We are constantly in search of happiness but, by our very natures, will not be able to find it permanently in either interpersonal relationships or creative work. Neither of these is the only way to happiness or invention or a happy future. The desire and pursuit of both, in the framework of the individual, is what leads us to those moments of elation and contentment.

This means grabbing them as soon as they appear and not waiting for the ideal. Living in the moment does not quite say it all, but certainly not always planning and using the spontaneity of opportunities as they appear is fundamental. This does take faith. Being spontaneous deliberately is an oxymoron, but acknowledging moments is a great start.

When the scientist or artist discovers a new truth 'outside', this becomes something with which they identify themselves, and therefore feel as 'inside'. Outer happenings and inner experience interact with each other, which is why when we hear a piece of music that touches us or see a movie that we relate to we experience this unity in our own heads.

Similarly, the process of reducing inner discord and reaching a degree of unification in our minds has a positive effect on our perception of the outside world.

The ability to hold an emotion in the space of inaction is revealing, relaxing and rewarding.

'Thoughts exist without a thinker'
W.R. Bion

We have a bad habit of holding on to thoughts, particularly the alienating ones. We hold on to them rather than feel them. We need to let the feeling flow rather than let it block all other feelings. As both Freudian and Buddhist teachings agree, it is our fear of experiencing ourselves directly that causes suffering.

If parts of ourselves remain denied, undigested or unintegrated, they become the points around which our defences and negative feelings collect. They are like black holes which absorb fear. If we tense up around the feelings we wish to deny, we end up only experiencing ourselves through our tensions: no wonder we feel bad ... hardly a good place to start having the confidence to create our future ...

When we can accept ourselves and tolerate and acknowledge our fears we begin to address the outer world with confidence, not anger or anxiety

So we can only have the courage to seize those moments when we accept ourselves

'We become much more free of other people, which in turn means that we become much more ourselves, our Real Selves, our authentic selves, our real identity'
Maslow

Maslow described the moments when we free ourselves of obligation, duty, fears and hopes as 'peak experience'. These are not confined to the people we generally regard as 'creative'. This is every person's right.

For most of us, new experiences are exciting but scary. Making the leap into the unknown demands exactly that, but there is no other way to do it. It also helps to know that no new experience is going to be, or can be, the ultimate. By our very natures all of our fascinations lie with continuing journeys, and it helps to know sometimes when trying to make that leap of faith that it is only a step on a journey, only one of many experiences, rather than *the* one. Spending our lives longing for the ultimate experience, or perfection, can only result in disappointment, disaffection and, above all, missed opportunities.

'Striving after originality takes you far away from your true self, and makes your work mediocre'
Keith Johnstone

Seen through this lens, all experiences become not only valuable but potential sources of excitement. This is how we begin to invent our future, by allowing it to happen ... Reading about spontaneity won't make it happen, or make you spontaneous, but it may stop you heading off in the opposite direction. Keith Johnstone suggests that there are three realisations to be attained before we can let go:

1. that we struggle against our imaginations, especially when we *try* to be imaginative;

2. that we are not responsible for the content of our imaginations; and

3. that we are not, as we are taught to think, our personalities, but that the imagination is the true self.

So we are often caught in a vicious circle of wanting to be ourselves but not allowing ourselves to let go and get in touch with it ...

Time for courage and faith.

Courage and faith is about accepting, not blocking. In our lives, when we get scared we say no, sometimes in very subtle ways. We are very skilled at suppressing spontaneity. Actors who are improvisers have the skill to accept and develop action. They accept whatever the other actors 'offer' them, and work with it. The energy released between improvising actors is enormous. It is also incredibly rewarding because it is directly in touch with each person's creative spirit.

the changing rooms

THE BUZZ FROM THAT CONNECTION IS SOMETIMES BETTER THAN AN AUDIENCE RESPONSE.

Effective group facilitators have to have the improviser within them in order to be able to accept the group 'offers' and not block them. They also need to give the group permission to let go in order to release their potential. To invent our own future, we need to be able to do these things for ourselves: to free ourselves to make and accept offers and not block; to release the energy needed to make that leap of faith.

There are those in this world who say 'yes', and there are those who say 'no'. Those who say 'yes' are sometimes rewarded with adventure and discovery; those who say 'no' are sometimes rewarded with safety and the status quo.

Inventing your future, by definition demands a 'yes' respondent, otherwise you would stay where you were. Maybe part of the delight and excitement with letting go is knowing when to say 'yes' and when to say 'no' ...

What would you say 'yes'

to now, at this moment?

What would you like to do right now,
more than anything else?

Why can't you do it?

BOLDLY GO …

Why is it that we tire so quickly of concepts that we initially embrace wholeheartedly, hopefully and completely? We welcome them but fail to translate them into reality: we then tire of our own failure, and blame the failure on the ideas. It isn't the ideas we have really tired of; it is our inability to make them come true and change things.

So why can't we translate them? Usually because we keep them at the level of concepts or ideas, and only look at them from an intellectual standpoint without imbuing them with any spirit or personal belief. The issues that we now believe are important such as values, empowerment, care for the environment, service and quality are all issues about personal values, not concepts. These are all things we care deeply about, and are tied to our soft squidgy bit ...

the changing rooms

**Things we care about we find harder to commit
to because the threat of failure means
so much more to us.**

**We will make and take decisions about things we care less for
without soul searching.**

What could be more important
to us than our own future?

It is hardly surprising that we find it so hard to make that leap ... We can pledge ourselves to the cause of teamwork, but if we don't believe in it nothing will happen ...

Having the courage and faith in ourselves is not an overnight project.

We cannot hope to invent our futures, or even realise our realities, without courage and faith.

All our fears and excitement are bound together deep in the darker recesses of our minds. They are a package; you don't get one without the other. Accepting our fears allows us to pull the inspirational trigger. We can touch them if we let go; if we stay aware and alert to the possibilities of the white space around us, and seize the moments when we feel them, not think them ...

'The range of what we think and do
is limited by what we fail to notice.
And because we fail to notice
that we fail to notice
there is little we can do
to change
until we notice
how failing to notice
shapes our thoughts and deeds'
R.D. Laing

RESOURCE GUIDE

the reality hacker's way through the universe and beyond....

This is not intended to be an exhaustive list of things you must do. It is a record of the things one reality hacker found stimulating and inspiring. Use it to spark off ideas and create your personal resource guide. Add to it as things happen to you.

– Make lists of people who you perceive to be reality hackers

  and talk to them

– Write down your dreams for a week

– Subscribe to (and read) *Scientific American* and *UTNE Reader*

– Leave your workspace in a mess every so often and then reorganise it

– Read *Le Petit Prince* by Antoine de Saint-Exupery (in English or

  French)

– Sing loudly

– Hide under the duvet

– Make a decision based only on gut feelings at least twice a month

– Visit Snoqualmie Falls

– Listen to your children

– Try writing with your wrong hand

– Read *Why zebras don't get ulcers* by Robert Sapolsky

– Watch and hear the Dalai Lama

– Spend days in bookshops

– See the film *The Princess Bride*

– Close your eyes and think of something to make you smile

– Read *My many coloured days* by Doctor Seuss

– Head for the mountains

– Visit the North West coast of Scotland

– Watch *Star Trek* and *Deep Space Nine*

– Spend an afternoon absorbed in the films *Jean de Florette* and

Manon Des Sources

– Wake up and do the first thing that comes into your head occasionally

– Read *You just don't understand* by Deborah Tannen

– Read *Mondo 2000*

– Mix yourself a smoothie with yogurt, banana and blueberries

(then drink it)

– Drink Peets coffee, particularly the Java

– Read *Understanding comics* by Scott McCloud

– Plant a tree for someone or even yourself

– Read *Living without a goal* by James Ogilvy

- Once a year try something you have never tried before (from cooking

   one-handed to caving)

- Watch *Il Postino* and *Cinema Paradiso*

- Read a selection of Margaret Atwood books

- Read at least one John Irving book

- Spend time staring into space

- Talk to plants

- Sit under trees

- Hug a rock

- Smile at people you don't know

- Spend time remembering . . .

- Keep track of yourself

- Watch improv artists

The need to use all the resources one has at one's disposal becomes crucial as we all have to do more with less. Missing or misinterpreting a verbal or non-verbal cue from someone can cost days of time, effort and misdirected-directed energy.

This is an example of something you might find useful.

So what is the formula for releasing and harnessing potential for growth?

Reaching **POTENTIAL** = Extending **REACH**

R	relate	asking questions, observing, listening
E	engage	checking understanding, show responsiveness
A	activate	interpret signs, set ideas in motion
C	connect	facilitating action
H	help	provide support and encouragement

Relate	observe, ask questions, listen and pick up signals and information
Engage	respond to signals and check on messages
Activate	interpret the signals and develop ideas and interventions
Connect	facilitate action and make things happen , sometimes without overt or obvious intervention
Help	be able to encourage and nurture whatever activity has been undertaken

We'd *still* love to know what inspires you and what you think of the book.
Please e-mail Nicola and us at *capstone_publishing@msn.com*.
We can't promise an immediate reply as Nicola travels extensively
but we will answer as reality permits.